Are you looking for cash?

Is your stock portfolio earning you 15 to 20% per year? If not then you need to read this book and learn how to make money with options on your stock portfolio. It is being done very successfully with the concepts and actual trading results provided here. The chart below is just one aspect of when to make an investment that pays off with excellent returns. It indicated on December 17, 2004 that it was Time to Act and invest. To be successful on a continuous basis you need much more then luck. You need a process the can be repeated over and over. It is all here in this book. Once you read it you will discover there is a way one can be very successful in generating CA$H for LIFE.

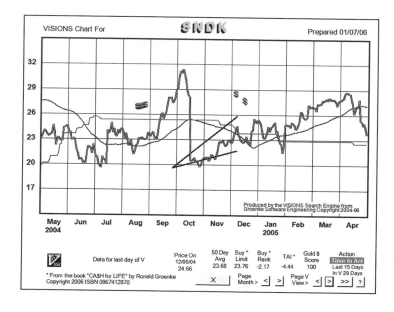

Comments from Investors

Excellent presentation at the seminar. I strongly recommend Ron's book, *Cash for Life* and VISIONS software. They are essential for finding solid stocks and profitable options.

Fred Anderson
Florida

Cash for Life is the book that, as a finance professor, I wish that I had written. Ron presents a methodology of capital market trading in a readable, understandable, and achievable manner. I have both presented his technique in the classroom and have adopted it personally. Simply stated, "Ron's methods really work." Thank you, Ron.

Harry F. Griffin Ph.D.
Assistant Professor of Finance
The University of Montevallo
Montevallo, Alabama

Ron Groenke patiently and in a down-to-earth manner explains very complex subject matter, namely selling stock options for conservative investors in his book *Cash for Life* and seminars. His VISIONS software is brilliant in making it easier to select particular stocks and options, and he is continuously updating it.

James Devenny (retired patent attorney)
Ottawa Canada

The book and seminar enhanced my understanding of covered calls and naked puts. I feel I can become more proactive in helping my husband manage our portfolio. *Cash for Life* is an essential book for any investor. VISIONS software is an absolute must!

Susan Wilhite
Arkansas

In writing *Cash for Life* Ronald Groenke has taken the road less traveled and produced a very practical guide to the conservative elements of options trading, and has done so in an easy to read and entertaining style. His story approach to the material removes the intimidation usually found in books on options trading. *Cash for Life* is a book I can comfortably recommend to my friends who are average investors. They will understand the material and will discover a relatively low-risk way of making money in the stock market, and may even find that they have made some new imaginary friends through the characters used in telling the option story.

Frederick P. Schadler, PhD
Associate Professor, Finance
College of Business
East Carolina University
Greenville, NC 27858

Ron Groenke's stock and options seminar is the perfect complement to his book *Cash for Life*. I feel I have gained additional insight into strategies that will enable me to improve on my financial goals. I highly recommend this to anyone interested in managing their own portfolios.

Darrel D. Smith
Baldwin, KS

I highly recommend *Cash for Life* by Ronald Groenke. It is an excellent supplemental text for finance couses. The book does a fine job of illustrating how writing options can be used to enhance the returns on a common stock portfolio. The real world context in which the story unfolds is a critical advantage, allowing students to observe a derivatives strategy in a practical application.

J. Howard Finch, Ph.D.
Associate Dean, Alico Chair in Finance
Lutgert College of Business
Florida Gulf Coast University
10501 FGCU Blvd., South
Fort Myers, Florida 33965-6565

I have bought very expensive investment software but Ron's VISIONS is the one I use. I just wish I had learned about VISIONS and the concepts in *Cash for Life* sooner. The VISIONS software is all that is needed for investing my money for retirement. I like the low risk and steady income aspect, whether the stock goes up or down. I started writing covered calls two weeks after reading the book and downloading the software.

Preston Brown
Charlotte NC

I have been using Ron's VISIONS software and strategy for about 6 months now, and am a believer that "slow and steady" does win the race. My monthly results have averaged out to be about twice the return of the S&P 500. I employ this strategy in several accounts and am seeing a monthly stream of income as a result. Even when negative news about a company results in downside movement in the stock, Ron's strategy limits the loss, and even resulted in a few gains. I'd like to thank Ron for introducing me to this straightforward, low-risk method of generating income with the stock market. I highly recommend *Cash for Life* to get you started making money on your portfolio.

Bill Datri
Parsippany, NJ

In his book *Cash for Life* Ron does an excellent job of showing a simple but effective way to trade covered calls. I just love his approach for this reason: It is a simple, easy to learn and conservative approach that I can trade in my IRA account. The companion software, VISIONS, is easy to navigate and does 95% of the work for me. Like Ron says . . . You make money by selling--not by buying."

LW - Birmingham, Al

More comments begin on pages 129 and 167.

CA$H
FOR LIFE

Unlock the Incredible
Monthly CASH Income
in your Stock Portfolio
by Mastering the Art of Selling
Covered Calls & Naked Puts
at the Right Time
on the Right Stocks

Ronald Groenke

KELLER PUBLISHING
Marco Island, Florida

ISBN 13: 978-0-9674128-7-0
ISBN 10: 0-9674128-7-0

Printed in the United States of America

Published by:

KELLER PUBLISHING
590 Fieldstone Dr.
Marco Island, FL 34145

www.KellerPublishing.com

*To my lovely wife Jean
who has been a great inspiration in all of my
endeavors and has brought me much happiness.*

Contents

Acknowledgment

Thanks to my friend, Wade Keller, who has also been my editor and publisher. It was at a Rotary Club meeting several years ago that I gave a presentation on my stock options strategy. After the meeting Wade said, "Ron, you've got a book there." That was the beginning of the process that led to this book.

I would also like to acknowledge and give heartfelt thanks to Wade's wife, Sue, for her interest and friendship.

Disclaimer

There is a high degree of financial risk when trading in the stock and options market. The author and publisher stress that it is possible to lose money that is invested in these markets. The methods and techniques presented in this book may be profitable or they may result in a loss. Past results are necessarily not indicative of future results. The examples of specific companies that are used in this book are only for informational purposes and are not recommendations.

This publication is sold with the understanding that the author and publisher are not engaged in providing legal, accounting, or other professional services. If legal advice or other expert assistance is required, the services of a competent professional should be sought. Although every precaution has been taken in the preparation of this book, the publisher and author assume no liability for errors and omissions. This book is published without warranty of any kind, either expressed or implied. Furthermore, neither the author nor the publisher shall be liable for any damages, either directly or indirectly arising from the use or misuse of the book.

Before investing, learn as much as you can about the investments that you plan to make. Do extensive research. Knowledge will put the odds in your favor.

Preface

Let's say you own some blue chip stock. Do you realize that you could sell a call option at a stock price higher than the current price and earn five to six percent on your holdings in three months or even ten percent in six months? There is no additional risk. You have already assumed the risk of stock ownership. After selling CALL options, if the stock goes up enough your stock gets called (you sell it) at a price you specified. If the stock stays about the same or goes down, the CALL option expires. In either case you pocket the money (premium) generated by selling the option.

Company/ Stock	Stock Price 1/23/06	Call Option Strike Month	Call Option Strike Price	Call Option Symbol	Call Option Premium	% Gain if Sold	% Gain if Expired
Intel	21.35	Apr	22.50	NQDX	0.70	8.67	3.28
(INTC)		Jul	22.50	NQGX	1.20	11.01	5.62
Boston Sci	23.34	May	25.00	BSXEE	1.25	12.47	5.36
(BSX)		Aug	25.00	BSXHE	1.95	15.47	8.35
Gen Elec	33.29	Jun	32.50	GEFZ	1.95	3.48	5.86
(GE)		Jun	35.00	GEFG	.70	7.24	2.10
Amer Pwr	23.05	Mar	22.50	PWQCX	1.50	4.12	6.51
(APCC)		Jun	22.50	PWQFX	2.20	7.16	9.54
Verisign	21.47	Mar	22.50	QVRCX	0.90	8.99	4.19
(VRSN)		Jun	22.50	QVRFX	1.70	12.72	7.92

In the chart above, second example, you could receive $1.25 per share on your Boston Scientific stock for an option lasting four months, expiring in May. That's a return of 12.47%. If you are willing to let the option expire in August you receive, immediately, $1.95 per share. The premium is yours regardless of whether the option expires or is exercised.

Perhaps you would like to buy a blue chip stock but not at the current price. Did you know someone would pay you while you wait for the price to go down? By selling a **PUT** option you pick the price and time frame for your willingness to invest. If the price of the stock goes down to your desired price you buy the stock. If the price stays about the same or goes up the **PUT** option expires. Again in either case you pocket the money (premium) generated by selling the option. A put option that is three months out could return four to five percent of the stock purchase price, or even eight percent for waiting six months.

Company/ Stock	Stock Price 1/23/06	Put Option Strike Month	Put Option Strike Price	Put Option Symbol	Put Option Premium	% Dis- count	New Stock Price if As- signed
Intel	21.35	Apr	20.00	NQPD	0.50	2.50	19.50
(INTC)		Jul	20.00	NQSD	0.85	4.25	19.15
Boston Sci	23.34	Feb	22.50	BSXNX	0.60	2.67	21.90
(BSX)		May	20.00	BSXQD	0.65	3.25	19.35
Gen Elec	33.29	Mar	32.50	GEOZ	0.55	1.69	31.95
(GE)		Jun	32.50	GERZ	0.90	2.77	31.60
Amer Pwr	23.05	Mar	20.00	PWQOD	0.20	1.00	19.80
(APCC)		Jun	20.00	PWQRD	0.60	3.00	19.40
Verisign	21.47	Mar	20.00	QVROD	0.60	3.00	19.40
(VRSN)		Jun	20.00	QVRRD	1.15	5.75	18.85

For example, considering Intel in the chart above you would receive $.50 for each share you agree to buy for $20.00 per share through expiration date in April. Of course you would only be "put" the stock if it is below $20.00 at the end of that period. In either case, as with calls, you receive and keep the premium. For Verisign you would receive $1.15 per share if you agree to be put the stock at a price of $20.00 per share through June expiration.

The concepts and techniques in this book have been proven in actual practice. The author has executed these types of transactions over the past twenty years and has the account history to back up the principles in this publication. Actual account trading results are given in Chapter 15 that demonstrate what is possible. These results can be reviewed as they are updated over time with new trades. See the VISIONS* software Now ScoreCards feature for further update details.

These concepts are available for anyone to use. The problem is that most investors, even most financial advisors, do not understand the advantage of using options to enhance portfolio performance. If the additional returns on your investment seem unreal after you have implemented some of the strategies in this book, great for you. You keep the rewards of your new investment skills and I have the satisfaction knowing that I was able to advance your financial well being.

* VISIONS is a unique stock and options search engine designed to get the information that allows you to make better informed investment decisions. It is available at the author's website: **RonGroenke.com**. A description can be found in the appendix.

Introduction

by Jerome Tuccille

Ronald Groenke has written a gem of a book that is ideal for conservative investors looking for low-risk opportunities in the options market. For most investors, the options market is an arcane universe populated by puts and calls, spreads and straddles, and other unfathomable concepts. The author has done an admirable job of de-coding the mysteries surrounding these investment products and rendering them comprehensible to average investors. Most people who are unfamiliar with options regard them as highly speculative and specialized tools for sophisticated investors. What is largely overlooked is that, for every free-wheeling investor who speculates on puts and calls, there is a conservative investor on the other side of the trade who uses options to generate extra income for his or her portfolio. *Ca$h for Life* addresses the conservative side of the options market.

This book offers one of the best expositions of low-risk options trading I've ever read. I was particularly impressed by the stock-picking advice and discourse on how to find value in puts and calls.

Also valuable is the so-called "Cedric Chart" on historical stock market highs and lows, which at first glance appears deterministic, but is primarily reflective of boom and bust cycles in the past and serves as a suggested roadmap for the future.

The author leads the reader by the hand through the basics of the most conservative options strategies, such as selling covered calls and selling puts on stocks one would like to own. By the time investors are finished absorbing the information contained in *Ca$h for Life*, they will feel comfortable embarking on the strategies discussed, with the goal of generating extra income in their accounts on a regular basis. As an investment professional with 30 years experience in the financial services industry, I wholeheartedly recommend this book.

Jerome Tuccille is the author of 21 books, including *How to Profit from the Wall Street Mergers*, *Rupert Murdoch*, and *Alan Shrugged*.

CA$H
FOR LIFE

1

The Money Tree

Why not go out on a limb. That's where the fruit is.
Will Rodgers

"Jake!" Katie Kimball finally got her husband's attention. Before selling Kimball CPA Firm and retiring to south Florida, Jake could be counted on to be out of the house and at the office at least 10 hours a day.

Looking up from the early edition of the *New York Times Book Review* Jake quietly replied, "Yes, dear?"

"I said, 'Are you going to Rotary today?' And now that I've got your attention would you mind not scattering your newspapers all over the floor. And by the way the Petersons are just back from the Alaska cruise. I saw Lori at Walgreens and she was driving a new BMW convertible. So cute. Their son has graduated from Bowdoin and is accepted at Harvard Law School. Now if you are going to Rotary I will press that new shirt I got for you at Goodwill. But if you are not going we should go walk on the beach because it's low tide now and you know. . ."

The phone rang and Jake quickly retreated again to the safe environment of the book reviews. Before he could find where he had left off the worrisome thoughts came again. He laid the paper down and looked out the window at the areca palms he had planted as a border across the back of their modest home only three blocks from the beach. He had sold the CPA firm too soon and for too little. In their mid fifties they had moved to the pleasant community of Marco Island with plans to write the Great American Novel and get it published before their savings ran out. A recent statement from their investment advisor had shown that funds in the retirement account were getting dangerously low. And unless he finished the novel, that was all they had to live on.

These thoughts were never far from his mind. His wife's comments about his new shirt from the Goodwill store and the conspicuous consumption by their friends, Lori and Steve Peterson, had caused his financial concerns to come roaring back to the surface. And now the old scar on his left arm began to ache. In his youth he had enjoyed surfing and had once been nipped by a small shark off the coast of Australia.

He needed to do something. Take action. He glanced quickly at his watch and his coffee cup. A command decision was required. Yes! Plenty of time for another cup of coffee before going to Rotary.

* * *

Jake stood in awe. Like an appreciative artist admiring a Rodin sculpture, he stood looking at the most beautiful new sports car he had ever seen. Long and powerful, it made a statement of elegant practicality. It had caught his attention as he was about to enter the Hideaway Beach Club for the Rotary luncheon. He enjoyed the Marco Island Rotary Club. It was a close-knit, fun group and he knew all the members. Several owned expensive cars. Al's Rolls Royce came to mind. He was curious wondering which of his friends had acquired the new beauty.

The invocation and pledge of allegiance to the flag were followed by introduction of guests. Looking across the room Jake saw his friend Steve Peterson stand up to introduce a guest who looked vaguely familiar. The visitor reminded him of a college professor from years ago. What was the name? Graham? Yes that was it. Professor Robert Graham. But that's not likely he thought. After all he hadn't seen the professor in over 30 years.

His mind easily slipped back to a particular scene from his college days. He had pulled frantically into the parking lot, already five minutes late for his first class of the semester. It was a hot fall day at the University of Minnesota. As he grabbed his books from the back seat he noticed another car jerk to a stop in the vacant slot next to him. Steam was billowing from under the hood and the car was generally

CHAPTER I | THE MONEY TREE

banged up. Jake noticed the windshield had a long crack. Apparently the driver's side door wouldn't open because the young man slid across the front seat and quickly out the passenger side with brief case in hand.

"Can I help you?" Jake had asked, concerned that the car might catch on fire.

Noticing Jake for the first time, the man quickly said, "Hi. Sorry, don't have time to chat. I'm running late for class. Old Betsy will be OK once she cools off. Powerful thirst." With that the man raced into the building.

As Jake made his way to the classroom he was surprised to see the owner of the old clunker standing at the lectern. Finding a seat Jake noticed the professor had a pleasant smile and twinkle in his eyes as he said to the class, "Welcome to Finance 101. My name is Robert Graham. Don't call me doctor yet as I still have a little work to do on my Ph.D. dissertation. Just call me professor."

Jake was jarred out of his trip down memory lane by the commanding baritone voice of Steve Peterson. "We have a former Rotarian. A Paul Harris Fellow. My special guest today has a suite on the same floor at my condominium. We met on the elevator this morning and, spur of the moment, I invited him to join us for lunch. Please give a warm Rotary welcome to a new resident of Marco Island, Dr. Robert Graham."

After the meeting Jake wasted no time in introducing himself to the professor. "Hi professor. Remember me? Jake Kimball. I was in your finance class at U of M, fall of 1975."

Rob shook hands and smiled as he searched his memory bank. So many students over a twenty-year teaching career. And now he had been retired from teaching for ten plus years.

"Hmmm. You say you were in my class at the University of Minnesota. That was actually my first teaching job. Wait a minute. Were you by chance the enterprising student who helped me get my car started after that first class? You had something you poured in the radiator to stop the leak. And then we used a bucket to get water and fill up the radiator."

Jake was smiling and nodding. "Yes, that was me. It was a good class, Finance 101, but as an Accounting major that was the only finance class I needed."

They continued talking as they walked out to the parking lot. Jake noticed they were heading in the direction of the new car he had admired earlier. His first thought was serious doubt that a former college professor could own such an expensive car. Then he remembered Steve Peterson's comment in introducing Rob. Steve and Lori lived in one of the two penthouse suites on the top floor of one of the most expensive condos on the beach. And Steve had said that Rob lived on the same floor. All of this went through his mind as they continued to talk and were soon standing next to the car.

Jake's look of amazement was obvious. Rob smiled and said, "This is Old Betsy. A little different from the one you helped me with."

"Professor I don't mean to be nosey but I've got to ask. What did you do, win the lottery?"

"No Jake, not the lottery. But I guess you could say I discovered a money tree." Rob paused and seemed lost in thought for a moment. Then he noticed that Jake was waiting patiently for more information, like the good student he had been many years before.

"Jake it was right under my nose all those years I was teaching finance. About 20 years ago I discovered a way of earning a high rate of return on my stock portfolio and generating current income with no additional risk or depletion of my portfolio. I call the concept CA$H for LIFE. As soon as I knew for sure it was working I retired from teaching and devoted all my time to investing. Say Jake it's good to see you. I'll probably be joining the club." Rob pulled out his PDA, pushed a button and the powerful engine purred smoothly as the driver's side door swung up and out of the way.

"But professor, wait. What did you mean by "money tree" and "high rate of return"? How can I learn more about this CA$H for LIFE?" Jake hoped he didn't sound desperate.

"Hmmm. Maybe it is about time I became a professor again. Let me make a quick call."

"Hello Jean. I'm going to be about 30 minutes late. I met an old friend at the Rotary meeting. Yes love. I love you too. Meet at the same place, thirty minutes later." Then he reached in his car and retrieved a notebook. "I have an example in here. Let's go back inside and sit down at a table."

Tiffany, the hostess, greeted them with a warm smile and escorted them to a secluded table when they explained their purpose. "You won't be disturbed here," she said. "Can I bring you tea or coffee?"

Jake felt a sense of high anticipation as Tiffany quickly set cups of herbal tea on the table. Finally Rob pulled a single sheet of paper out of his notebook, looked at the paper and looked at Jake. Then he slid the single sheet of paper across the table.

2

Covered Calls

A genius is a talented person who does his homework.
Thomas A. Edison

"Jake what I am about to show you is very simple and yet very power-ful. I've only got time to give you a quick overview right now. I promise we will get together again. In fact if you are really interested I'll give you a homework assignment. Here, take a look at an investment I made in Interdigital Communications (IDCC). IDCC is one of the leading companies that provide technology for wireless communica-tions. If you have a cell phone one of their integrated circuits may be inside.

The paper contained the following table:

INTERDIGITAL COMMUNICATIONS	IDCC	DAQ	MAR	JUN	SEP	DEC			
11-24-03	B		1000		20.29	20295.00	-20295.00	
11-24-03	S	10	DEC	20.00	1.30	1279.93	-19015.07	CE
12-22-03	S	10	MAR	20.00	2.35	2329.89	-16685.18	CE
03-22-04	S	10	JUN	20.00	.65	629.97	-16055.21	CE
06-21-04	S	10	SEP	20.00	.95	929.97	-15125.24	CE
09-20-04	S	10	JAN	20.00	.75	729.98	-14395.26	CE
01-24-05	S	10	MAR	20.00	1.00	979.96	-13415.30	CE
03-21-05	S	10	JUN	20.00	.90	794.92	-12620.38	CE
06-20-05	S	10	AUG	20.00	1.15	1129.95	-11490.43	CE
08-22-05	S	10	DEC	20.00	1.00	979.95	-10510.48	CE
12-19-05	S	10	MAR	20.00	.70	684.97	-9825.51	CO
03-17-06	P		1000		20.00	19980.00	10154.49	<

Rob remained silent. After a couple of minutes Jake looked up.
"Professor, I believe I understand part of the first line. On Novem-

8

ber 24, 2003 you bought 1000 shares of IDCC at $20.29 a share. But I'm not sure I understand the last two columns. Where did the 20295.00 come from? And why do the numbers in the last column go from negative to positive?"

"This is my short hand way of keeping up with my investments," explained Rob. "I have developed a software program that analyzes each of my investments as part of my overall portfolio. My primary concern is cash flow. I don't like to lose money. On each investment my first objective is to have a positive cash flow. My second objective is to have a *very* positive cash flow. But more about CA$H for LIFE later. First let's make sure you understand the basics here.

"You are correct that I bought 1000 shares of IDCC. The price per share was $20.29. I use a discount, on-line broker and the sales commission was $5.00. Add the sales commission of $5.00 to the purchase of 1000 shares at $20.29 a share and you have my total cash outflow. For this one purchase my total cash outflow was $20,295.00. The next to the last column is the transaction amount and the last column is a running total or the cumulative effect of all the transactions. Since this was a cash outflow the dollar amount is shown as a negative.

"But now let's take a look at the second line of the IDCC chart. On the same day that I bought the 1000 shares, I sold 10 contracts of December calls at a strike price of $20.00. The S in the first column means I made a sale. In the next column the "10 DEC 20.00" tells me what I sold. One contract is for 100 shares, the minimum needed to sell an option. So my 1000 shares of stock allow me to sell 10 contracts. That means that at the time the market price of IDCC was $20.29 a share I sold the option for someone to buy my 1000 shares for $20.00 a share any time up until the close of the market on the third Friday the following December. $20.00 is the strike price. If the market price drifts below $20.00 it will not be profitable for the buyer of the option to buy my shares for $20.00. Only if the market price stays above $20.00 will it be profitable for the option buyer to exercise the option. The price I received for that option was $1.30 per share. Less commission that came to $1279.93.

"Notice that the transaction amount, next to last column, is positive. Selling the call means I received money so it is a cash inflow. That has the effect of reducing the cumulative balance in the last column. At this point my net investment is $19,015.07 for the 1000 shares of IDCC.

"My strategy here is called a covered call. That means I owned the stock, 1000 shares of IDCC, and on those shares I sold a call option. It's called a "covered" call because, in the event the stock is called, I'm already covered. I already own the stock and can readily hand it over. The purchaser of the option has the right, but not the obligation, to purchase my 1000 shares for $20.00 a share anytime up to the close of the market on December 19, 2003. I received the premium of $1,279.93 for selling that right or option. Now the purchaser can be expected to exercise the option if the market price of IDCC stays above $20.00 during that time period. It could be exercised anytime before expiration but most likely the option would not be exercised until the last day of the option period. Of course it would be foolish to exercise the option if the market price is below $20.00. One would buy at the current market price rather then buying my stock for $20.00.

"As it turned out the call option was not exercised. See the "CE" at the end of line two. CE stands for "Call Expired."

Jake was beginning to see an entirely new concept in stock ownership. "Hmmmm," he began, "you are actually generating a stream of income just from owning stocks. Do many people do this? I don't think I've heard about it before. I've got a lot of questions. Are there many stocks that you can do this with? What kind of investment return can you make?

"Hold on Jake. First let me ask you a few questions. Maybe it would be best if you told me your impression of the stock market." Rob's professorial techniques were kicking in.

Jake and Katie had most of their funds invested in the stock market. They were in mutual funds managed by their investment advisor. Jake thought for a moment before responding.

"Individual stocks go up and down. Over time most of the stocks go up more than they go down so the overall market goes up gradually over time. The market is risky because some stocks go down more than up and may even end up worthless. We have our investments diversified in mutual funds to minimize the risks. That's about all I know. Well I guess I could add what my investment advisor says. His name is Nicholas Abbott. According to Nicholas your best strategy is to just sit tight for the long haul. Don't try to time the market. Don't worry about the ups and downs because over the long haul it will be up. And of course, his main advice, *trust Nicholas* to put us in decent mutual funds.

"As for options," Jake continued, "I've always heard of people buying options and that's a gamble that the stock will shoot up. If it does you make a lot of money. But I always thought of that as gambling, like playing blackjack in Vegas. It never occurred to me that people actually sell options."

Rob nodded. "That's a pretty good analysis of the market, Jake. And you are right, a lot of people buy stock options hoping the underlying stock will shoot up. But it is much more likely that the stock will move in a narrow range in a short period of time. My motto is *'You make money by selling, not by buying'*.

"Here's my pocket calculator and your first test for this semester. What was my return on investment from selling those ten contracts on November 24, 2003? By the way one contract is for 100 shares of stock."

Jake eagerly took the calculator and began solving the problem. He decided that the return for selling the call was $1,279.93. Now what should be the investment base to divide into the return? Well apparently the total cash outflow of $20,295.00. Dividing the former by the later he got 6.31%. He started to state the answer but then the thought occurred: over what time period. He smelled a trap. Sure, 6.31% was a good return but that was for less than a year. What was the APR, annual percentage rate? How many days from November 24, 2003 to December 19, 2003? A quick count gave him 25 days. So to annualize the return he multiplied 6.31% by 365 and divided by 25.

Looking at the professor he said, "92.13% sir."

"Very good Jake. Actually I never bother to annualize. I have another technique that I'll tell you about later. I'm satisfied with a good, quick return. Just for the heck of it why don't you compute the return for line three."

Jake quickly noted that the premium per share for the next sell of ten call contracts was $2.35 per share. After commissions Rob had netted $2,329.89. Now what was the amount of investment at that time? Presumably $19,015.07. He quickly made the computation.

"I get 12.25 % without annualizing. However annualizing would be fairly simple. It took three months to earn the 12.25 %. So just quadruple it for the APR. Either way it's a darn good return.

"I'm beginning to get the hang of this. The CE on the end of your net investment on line three means the call expired so you were able to do it again. I'll compute the gain on line four. Let's see. You again sold 10 contracts, this time at $.65 per share. After commissions you netted $629.97. By the way Professor when do you get this money?"

"It goes immediately into my brokerage account. I can take it out and spend it or I can invest it. The choice is mine. I earned it by selling the option."

Jake was amazed as the concept sunk in. "So this really is 'new money'. You have earned money on your portfolio but it's not capital gains and it's not dividends. I had no idea you could do this."

Rob smiled. He always enjoyed seeing the light come on with his students as he explained a new financial concept.

"Very good. Now here's another question for you. Most investment advisors say the way to make money in the stock market is to buy good stocks and hold for long-term appreciation. That's apparently the plan your investment advisor is following. How much of my return on IDCC was a result of stock appreciation or dividends?"

Jake knew better than to make a snap response. He looked closely at the chart again.

INTERDIGITAL COMMUNICATIONS IDCC DAQ MAR JUN SEP DEC								
11-24-03	B		1000		20.29	20295.00	-20295.00	
11-24-03	S	10	DEC	20.00	1.30	1279.93	-19015.07	CE
12-22-03	S	10	MAR	20.00	2.35	2329.89	-16685.18	CE
03-22-04	S	10	JUN	20.00	.65	629.97	-16055.21	CE
06-21-04	S	10	SEP	20.00	.95	929.97	-15125.24	CE
09-20-04	S	10	JAN	20.00	.75	729.98	-14395.26	CE
01-24-05	S	10	MAR	20.00	1.00	979.96	-13415.30	CE
03-21-05	S	10	JUN	20.00	.90	794.92	-12620.38	CE
06-20-05	S	10	AUG	20.00	1.15	1129.95	-11490.43	CE
08-22-05	S	10	DEC	20.00	1.00	979.95	-10510.48	CE
12-19-05	S	10	MAR	20.00	.70	684.97	-9825.51	CO
03-17-06	P		1000		20.00	19980.00	10154.49	<

"Professor you told me that CE stands for Call Expired. There are nine CE's and then a CO. What does CO stand for?"

"CO stands for Call Open. Notice the last column of the second to last line is -9825.51 CO. That means that on December 19, 2005 the call option was open. The owners of the call option have yet to exercise their rights. They have until March 17, 2006 to buy my 1000 shares for $20 a share.

You can see by the balance in the last column that my profit for this investment will be $10,154.49 if the stock is sold. So now you should be able to tell me how much of my profit is from stock appreciation or dividends."

Jake thought for another moment as he analyzed the chart. Finally he said, "You bought the 1000 shares for $20.29 each and are willing to sell them for $20 each. That's a twenty-nine cent per share loss. All of your return was from selling call options ten times. Apparently none of your return was from dividends. I would say you made nothing from stock appreciation. But there will be a profit of $10,154.49 if your stock is called. So, lets see, we have $10,154.49 divided by 20295.00 which is 50.03 % in roughly 28 months or 21.44 % per year. "

"That's right," said Rob. "I think of it as picking money from a money tree like you would pick fruit from, say, an orange tree. I tend to do short term option sales, pick some dollars and hope to get called. I don't mind if the stock shoots up and the option buyer makes a profit. Usually the option expires and I can pick some more fruit from the same tree. In this example I picked cash ten times from the money tree and added it to my CA$H for LIFE account. I'm happy with a good return every few months.

As the professor began to gather his papers Jake was thinking fast.

"But wait a minute," Jake exclaimed. "There has got to be a catch. This is too good to be true. What if you are picking fruit as the price of the stock is headed down?"

"Good point. And it can happen. In fact I think I have another example here that illustrates just that experience." Rob pulled a sheet of paper out of his note book and handed it to Jake. "Cott Corporation is a soft drink bottler. You can see that its stock price went from $9.50 a share down to $3.81 a share. During that time I picked so much fruit from the tree I made a profit of $9,847.80 even though I finally sold the stock at a loss.

"There is a definite risk in owning stock," Rob continued. "But that risk can be greatly mitigated, and in some cases even overcome, by selling calls. This particular investment reminds me of a small town in Minnesota. Have you ever heard of the town of Andover?"

Jake's head was reeling as he was still analyzing the sheet of paper detailing Rob's investment in Cott. He was counting the number of times calls had been sold on this one investment. He just managed to look up and mumble, "No, don't think so."

COTT CORPORATION COTTF CQT FEB MAY AUG NOV								
11-08-94	B		1500		9.5000	14279.00	-14279.00	
11-08-94	S	15	MAY	10.00	1.5625	2298.67	-11980.33	CE
11-30-94	B		1500		10.0000	15029.00	-27009.33	
11-30-94	S	15	MAY	10.00	1.7500	2579.91	-24429.42	CE
05-22-95	S	30	NOV	10.00	.9375	2742.40	-21687.02	CE
02-09-95	B		2000		9.6200	19279.00	-40966.02	
02-09-95	S	20	AUG	10.00	1.3750	2694.90	-38271.12	CE
08-22-95	S	20	NOV	10.00	.6250	1199.95	-37071.17	CE
11-15-95	S	50	MAY	10.00	.6250	3024.89	-34046.28	CE
05-20-96	S	50	NOV	10.00	.7500	3649.87	-30396.41	CE
11-18-96	S	50	MAY	10.00	.4375	2087.42	-28308.99	CE
05-19-97	S	50	AUG	10.00	.6250	3024.89	-25284.10	CE
08-18-97	S	20	NOV	10.00	.6250	1199.95	-24084.15	CE
08-18-97	S	30	NOV	10.00	.5625	1637.44	-22446.71	CE
11-24-97	S	50	FEB	10.00	.7500	3649.87	-18796.84	CE
02-24-98	S	50	MAY	10.00	.6250	3024.89	-15771.95	CE
05-15-98	S	50	AUG	7.50	.5000	2397.41	-13374.54	CE
08-25-98	S	50	NOV	7.50	.5000	2397.41	-10977.13	CE
11-17-98	S	50	MAY	7.50	.3750	1772.43	-9204.70	CE
06-23-99	S		5000		3.8100	19052.50	9847.80	<

"The story of how the town got its name is interesting. The Great Northern Railroad had a stop at a small northern town in the late nineteen twenties. One morning there was a derailment and the train rolled over and over and over. This accident was such a big news story the residents decided to rename the town Andover, to capture the event forever in history. I'm reminded of the name, Andover, when I sell calls over and over."

Jake was still full of questions as Rob's phone rang. "Yes Jean. I'm on the way. I'll see you in 10 minutes."

Looking at Jake he said, "Good thing this is a small island. OK you've learned a lot. Now here's your homework assignment. Get a copy of the Investors Business Daily. Go to the options page and pick three stocks that you are familiar with. I want you to assume a purchase of 100 shares of stock and sale of one covered call contract. Pick an option where the strike price—that is the price for which you are committed to sell—is close to the market price. Don't worry this will all become clear when you do the exercise. Remember once you've bought the stock you have assumed the risk of stock ownership. What you are doing by selling calls is generating income, "picking dollars off the money tree." You should be taking notes by the way.

"Here's a sheet of paper. Let's start over. First go to the options page. Your local paper may also have an options page. Or go to Yahoo Finance on the Internet, enter a stock symbol for a price quote and then select options. You will find option prices for both calls and puts. For now just concentrate on calls. Pick three stocks. Now for each stock pick four different call option contracts. The four options on each stock will differ by strike price or expiration date. Notice how the first IDCC option I sold was designated. It reads 10 Dec 20.00. That means the strike price is $20 for the 10 contracts. Options expire on the third Friday of each month. Since this a Dec option in 2003 the expiration date is December 19. I suggest you select for analysis four different call option contracts for each stock.

"Using IDCC again as an example, I sold Dec 20. Others that I considered were Dec 22.50, Mar 20.00, and Mar 22.50. Do you see what I am saying? Look at options from the standpoint both of strike price and expiration date. Since we are considering two strike prices and two expiration dates we have four possible combinations. Now compute the return for each of the four contracts assuming first CE and then CA. Those are the only two things that can happen. Either the call will expire, CE, or the call will be assigned, CA. Compute your return both ways. You will be making a total of 12 computations, four for each of the three stocks.

"You might as well write down the formulas for computing the return. They are:

$$\text{If Sold} = \frac{(\text{Strike Price} + \text{Premium} - \text{Purchase Price})}{\text{Purchase Price}}$$

$$\text{If Expired} = \frac{\text{Premium}}{\text{Purchase Price}}$$

"You'll be surprised how much you learn just doing this exercise."

Jake was writing furiously on the sheet of paper. He looked up to see the professor headed for the door.

"Professor, I've got questions. And when will you check my homework?"

Rob's cell phone rang before he got to the door. Opening the phone and looking over his shoulder at Jake he said, "I'll come back to Rotary next week. See you then."

And he was gone.

3

Take Control

Failure is the opportunity to begin again, more intelligently.
Henry Ford

"Katie my love, you are not going to believe who I met at Rotary today." Jake arrived home in a state of excitement with his newly purchased copy of the Investors Business Daily.

"Let me guess," replied Katie with a sly smile. "Could it possibly have been Rob Graham, the Finance Professor you had in college?" As Jake's mouth hung open she continued.

"I've just been on the phone with Lori. Steve is rather perturbed with you. He says you shanghaied his guest before he could introduce him to the membership chair and the president. According to Lori the only way we can make up for your outrageous indiscretion is for us to come over for cocktails and sunset on their balcony. So I accepted. Is that alright?"

"Sure. You know I'm always glad to visit with Steve and Lori. Besides I need to pick Steve's brain. He retired near the top of that big brokerage firm. With all the money they have he must have done really well as a stockbroker, or analyst, whatever he was. But right now I've got homework to do. I'm computing how much money we can make by selling covered calls."

"Covered who? Oh never mind. Just let me know when I can read another chapter of your novel. I'm anxious to find out how your *Walter Mitty* CPA character saves the nation from financial ruin."

As Jake did his computations he became increasingly familiar with the operations of the options market. Several points became obvious. Apparently there were three factors in his decision process which determined the amount of premium he could receive by selling a call option.

First, the time period to the expiration date was important. The premium offered for one month was not as great as the premium offered for three months or six months. The longer the option was in effect the more it was worth. He also noticed the "time value" of money come into play. A six month option, while more than a three month option, was less than twice the value; a three month option, worth more than a one month option, was less than three times the value.

The second factor under his control was the selection of the strike price. If a stock were selling for $12.50, a strike price of $15 would pay less than a strike price of $10. That made sense because with a $15 strike price the stock would have to rise more than $2.50 before the option would be exercised. A strike price of $10 meant the stock was already $2.50 above the price at which it could be bought by the option holder. A strike price of $10 meant the option already had $2.50 of intrinsic value in addition to its time value.

The third factor was the particular stock that he selected. Jake found two stocks that had the same closing price the previous day. When he checked the option premium for each, using the same strike price and expiration date, he found that stock A would yield a significantly higher premium than stock B. Maybe that had something to do with the volatility of the stock.

That would bear checking out.

He began to formulate some questions for the professor. First how do you know which stocks to buy? Is it just random or is there a way to wisely select stocks? Second how do you know which strike price and time period to choose? He began to suspect that once he had those questions answered there would be more questions. Also what was the deal with puts? He noticed that the stocks had both put and call options. He was deep in thought when Katie came over and pulled on his ear lobe.

"Let's go for a walk, handsome, and you can tell me how much money we are going to make with that covered stuff. We'll need to get back in plenty of time to make sunset with Steve and Lori."

* * *

"Jake, I'll bet you were surprised to see Rob. I had no idea you two knew each other." Jake and Katie had enjoyed a vigorous walk on the beach, showered and changed before going to the Peterson's penthouse condo for sunset and cocktails. Steve was in a bombastic mood. He had already extolled the virtues of his favorite sports teams and denigrated the lack of virtue of certain local political figures.

"Yes," Jake replied. "I was very pleasantly surprised. Rob Graham was my Finance Professor over thirty years ago. He had a certain presence in the classroom; you might say charisma that makes him easy to remember."

"You'll notice," Steve interrupted because this was his favorite time of day, "that the bottom of the sun has just touched the Gulf of Mexico. It will be exactly two minutes and forty six seconds until the sun is completely down. And I would say the conditions are good for a green flash this evening. Humidity is high and there are only a few clouds near the horizon."

The green flash was a popular topic of conversation. It occurred rarely and would only happen when the last of the sun dipped into the sea. Perhaps one time in a hundred a green flash could be seen just at that moment of last sunlight. You could consider yourself lucky if you saw it once. But of course the Petersons had seen it numerous times with their front row seat.

"Speaking of green," Jake piped in, "what do you think of making money in the options market?"

"You will lose your shirt," Steve replied with conviction. "You might as well go to Vegas and play the crap table. In my thirty years on Wall Street I never knew anyone to consistently make money buying options. It's just a gamble."

"Steve I never did understand exactly what you did on Wall Street."

"I started off as a broker. And then I managed one of our branch offices with about 50 brokers. So we were basically in sales. I would have clients occasionally who would insist on playing the options market. After they lost all they could afford I would then get them into some good solid companies for long term growth. I tell you, people who think they can manage their own money in the stock market, why that's like trying to operate on yourself. There are some things that just need to be handled by professionals and the stock market is one of them. My clients over the years would just turn every thing over to me. They didn't want to be bothered with the decisions. And of course my job was to preserve their capital. I guess you could say my motto was 'preserve and grow slowly'. And it paid off. We've been retired for fifteen years now, enjoying the good life.

"You know the old 80-20 rule. It's formally called the Pareto Principle after the Italian economist who discovered that generally 80% of the wealth was owned by 20% of the people. But it applies to a lot more than just wealth distribution. For example 80% of my problems came from the 20% of my clients who were always coming up with a hot stock tip or strategy, like the ones who wanted to gamble in the options market. I would give those clients to new trainees and keep the satisfied clients. All brokers like clients who appreciate their knowledge and expertise. Leave the driving to us, so to speak."

Steve leaned back in the lounge chair and smiled contentedly, enjoying the warm breeze, commanding view of the beach and the gulf. Four pelicans gracefully flew by. There were sailboats in the distance. The clouds were just right to pick up a red tint from the sun.

"But what if, Steve, instead of buying options, you sold options. And suppose further that you only sold options on stock that you already owned. Would that not be risk free income?"

Steve was about to take a sip of his margarita, Lori's specialty. Lori liked to brag that she had learned the secret recipe after chatting with the bartender at a local Mexican restaurant. The glass had reached Steve's lips and seemed to be frozen there. Time stood still. Finally Steve set the glass down and absent-mindedly licked the salt off his lips. His voice was usually a little on the loud side. But now it was low, just barely audible. He seemed almost to be talking to himself. "Hmmm. Sell options on stock that you own. Yes that would seem to work. Maybe that's why so many people buying options lose money. It's because people selling options are making money. If the stock goes up above the strike price you sell at a profit. You get the premium and part of the stock appreciation. If the stock goes down you still keep the premium. Psychologically you are not that concerned that the stock goes up right away. Long term sure you want it to go up and, if you pick a good stock, it will. But if the stock goes down you could buy the option back for pennies on the dollar and sell it again when the stock goes back up. Or just wait for the option to expire and then sell a new contract on the same stock. What's the risk? Well the stock price could move up sharply and your gain on the up side would be limited. But that rarely happens. Stocks move up over time but over short periods like three months, they mostly just move up and down within a narrow range. Of course the real risk is that the stock could go down. But you have that risk whether you sell options or not. So if you mean by 'risk free income' no additional risk then . . . "

Steve interrupted his rambling monologue and shouted to Lori, "Honey, would you bring me the Investors Business Daily." And then to Jake, "I wonder what kind of premium I could get on my portfolio? Why you know the more I think about it the more obvious it is. Hardly any stocks pay a decent dividend any more. The portfolio is just sitting there. And I'm sitting here hoping the market will go up a little bit. I've got dozens of stocks that have been virtually flat over the past couple of years. Might as well generate a little income while they're sitting there. Jake let me fix you another drink. Lori, did you throw out the papers?"

Jake noticed that the sky had become even more beautiful after the sunset. He smiled, looking forward to his next meeting with the professor.

4

You Make Money by Selling—Not by Buying

*The hardest struggle of all is to be something
different from what the average man is.*
Charles M. Schwab

Tiffany smiled when she saw Rob and Jake headed her way. "What are you guys doing here today? Rotary's not until Thursday." Tiffany had run on the college track team with Jake's daughter and fell in love with Marco Island while visiting on spring break. She and Jake were good friends and always kidded each other.

"Urgent business," Jake responded. "I'm learning how to plant a money tree. And if you give us good service I may show you how to plant one too." At Jake's request Rob had agreed to meet on Monday afternoon for a spot of tea and another investment lesson.

Tiffany seated them at a secluded table and went for the tea. Jake opened a folder in which he had his homework assignment and a series of questions.

"Professor, I hardly know where to start. Over the past 30 years I've generally invested any surplus funds in the market. But it's always been a straight investment and I generally just relied on the advice of my stock broker or a hot tip I got from a client. And I had a mutual fund IRA that I made regular contributions to. But after our discussion last week and the homework assignment I see a whole new possibility for earning income on a portfolio. I guess my key question is how to select stocks. Is it just random or is there a way to improve the odds. And also while I now have some understanding of selling calls I don't have a clue about puts. Are puts part of the CA$H for LIFE strategy. And there's the matter of . . ."

"Jake hold on." Rob grinned as Tiffany poured hot water on the herbal tea bag in each cup. "One step at a time.

Tiffany affectionately smoothed his slightly graying hair and said, "I overheard part of what you two were talking about last week." Turning to Rob and holding out her hand she said, "By the way, I'm Tiffany. Welcome to Marco Island."

"Thank you Tiffany. The hospitality is great and the weather is terrific. Are you interested in investments?"

"Oh yes. I joined an investment club. We're members of **NAIC**. There are 20 of us pooling $50 a week. So far at our meetings no one has mentioned options. I wonder if you would be willing to make a presentation."

Just then two couples entered the restaurant area of the club. "Got to go. I'll be back," as she bustled off.

"She's a great kid," Jake commented. "And a real hustler. I've never seen a young person with such eclectic interests. She writes articles for the local paper, coaches a young girls volleyball team and frequently is in plays produced by Marco Players our community theater group. And now, by golly, she's interested in investments."

"But professor," Jake continued. "Where do we go from here? I want to learn it all. But I know what you said is important. 'One step at a time'."

"I've given that some thought," Rob began. "Here's the order in which we should proceed:

"First, we should complete what I call *the money tree concept*. This is the process of selling—with emphasis on selling, not buying—options, both calls and puts. Last week we talked about calls. Today I will explain puts. Even though you will soon understand calls and puts, you will not be ready to execute a trade until you have fully mastered the next three lessons.

"Second, we need to build a prospect list of stocks. The key here is which stocks you allow onto your prospect list. Not all stocks are equal. I have developed definite criteria. Not complicated, just seven basic tests that a stock must pass before it is allowed on my list. Those seven tests protected me from the debacle known as the internet bubble.

"Third, once the prospect list is in place we need to rank the stocks on the list before deciding on an investment. I have developed two formulas for this. One is the Buy Limit which tells us the maximum price that you would pay for a stock. And the second is the Buy Rank which ranks the stocks based on their relative attractiveness. The formulas are not really complicated but it can get cumbersome if you are dealing with say 50 or 100 stocks on the prospect list. So I have developed a software program called **VISIONS** that accesses the Internet for stock data and allows you to sort your list, based on Buy Rank, or any other criteria, with just a few key strokes.

"Fourth, and finally, we come to execution. There are specific steps as well as record keeping I recommend in executing the order."

Rob paused for a sip of tea. It had gotten cool. As if reading his mind Tiffany appeared with fresh hot cups for both of them.

Jake was taking notes. Two competing thoughts were going through his mind: *Why didn't I know about this sooner?* And *Perhaps I can become master of my own investments!*

"I'm ready," he said hoping it didn't sound like a plea. "Let's take the next step."

Rob slid a chart across the table and turned it so Jake could read it.

	CALLS		
	Buy a Call You have the right to purchase a stock at a specified price for a certain period of time.	**Write (sell) a Call** You have an obligation to sell a stock at a specified price for a certain period of time, if the buyer activates the Call.	
BUY	**Buy a Put** You have the right to sell a stock at a specified price for a certain period of time.	**Write (sell) a Put** You have a obligation to buy a stock at a specified price for a certain period of time, if the buyer activates the Put	SELL
	PUTS		

"Calls and puts can be bought and sold," Rob explained. "That gives four possible transactions. There are many exotic strategies that make use of various combinations of these four basic transactions. I've examined and used most if not all of them. From my experience your best results will come from the right side of the chart. Remember my motto: ***You make money by selling not by buying.***

"Selling a put option means you incur the same risk as owning the stock on which you sell the put. Typically you will sell a put with a strike price less than the current price of the stock. If the stock goes down you are obligated to buy it at the strike price which may at that time be higher than the current stock price. If the stock goes up or remains about the same during the option period, the put will expire.

"What the buyer of the put option gets is the right to sell you that stock at the strike price until the option period expires. Investors buying puts are gaining insurance against the possibility that the stock will take a dive. You on the other hand, the seller of the put, have done your homework on the stock and are reasonably confidant it is staying relatively flat or going up. We'll get into stock selection later.

"Are you with me so far?"

Jake had been listening carefully and taking notes. "Yes I think so. One thing I like about the covered calls is that in a sense it is risk free. Of course owning stock is not risk free. It can always go down and you have a loss. But once you own the stock there is no additional risk associated with the call option. Either the option will expire or you will sell the stock at a price you have agreed to. But that doesn't seem to be the case with puts."

"That's right," Rob agreed. "At least that's the way I do it. Some people sell call options naked, that is without owning the stock. There is tremendous risk in that strategy. If the stock shoots up in price you could be forced to pay that high price for the stock and then immediately sell it at the lower strike price to comply with the option you sold. Naked calls are very risky. There's no limit to how high the stock could go, even if only temporarily, and create for you a tremendous loss. I always sell covered calls and never naked calls.

"Now with puts it's a little different. A covered put means selling a put on a stock that you have already sold short at the same strike price. So if you are forced to buy the stock you are just closing your short position. The money you earned by selling the put is eaten up by the transaction of selling the stock short and then buying it back. And of course if the stock goes up the put option expires but you lose money on the short sell of the stock. The higher the stock goes the more you lose. Covered puts are not appealing to me. Perhaps I'm just an optimistic bull and like to design a strategy based on the market going up.

"So in the case of puts I sell naked puts. There is risk of course. But at least the risk is limited in that the stock can not go below zero. That's not true of a naked call where the stock theoretically has no upper limit. The way I look at a naked put is this. Either the stock will go up and the option expires or the stock goes down and I get to buy a desired stock at a discount. If the later happens I analyze the stock again to make sure it is still desirable and then sell a covered call on my new stock acquisition."

Jake was taking notes and absorbing the concept of covered calls and naked puts. As he lay the pen down he slowly rubbed the scar on his arm from the shark bite, recalling his surfing incident years ago. "Professor, I think I need a picture."

"OK. Take a look at this transaction. It's one of my typical naked puts."

Rob again slid a single sheet of paper across the table.

5

The Naked Put

A man without financial surplus is controlled by circumstances,
whereas a man with financial surplus controls his circumstances.

Harvey Firestone

CAREER EDUCATION			CECO	CUY	JAN	APR	JUL	OCT	
12-06-04	S	10	DEC	30.00	.25	229.99	229.99		PE
12-20-04	S	10	JAN	30.00	.80	779.98	1009.97		PE
01-06-05	S	10	FEB	30.00	.50	479.98	1489.95		PE
02-09-05	S	10	MAR	35.00	.90	879.97	2369.92		PE
02-14-05	S	10	FEB	35.00	.65	629.97	2999.89		PE
06-06-05	S	10	OCT	25.00	.75	729.96	3729.85		PE
06-13-05	S	10	JUL	30.00	.75	229.98	3959.83		PE
07-11-05	S	10	AUG	30.00	.35	329.98	4289.81		PE
07-15-05	S	10	AUG	35.00	.70	679.97	4969.78		PE
08-22-05	S	10	JAN	30.00	1.30	1279.95	6249.73		PO
11-08-05	S	10	APR	25.00	1.05	1034.95	7284.68		PO

After a few moments Rob said, "Sometimes you get lucky and never have the naked puts assigned. Here is such an example with Career Education (**CECO**). Career Education Corporation provides post secondary education primarily in the United States.

"Tell me what you see."

Jake had been studying the chart intently for several minutes. "This may be too good to be true. There's got to be a catch here somewhere. What am I missing?

"Well," Jake continued, "I remember from the covered call chart on **IDCC** that each line represents a transaction. So on Dec 6, 2004 you sold puts on 10 contracts, 1000 shares, of **CECO**. **DEC** 30 means the strike price is $30 and the option will expire or be exercised on the third Friday in December. If the stock price is below $30 the holder of the option will require you to buy his 1000 shares for $30. If the stock price is above $30 the option will expire, which is apparently what happened. PE must stand for put expired. In exchange for selling that option you received $.25 per share or $229.99 net of commission. You continued doing that, selling naked puts on CECO, and over a twelve month period, December to the following November, earned $7,284.68. How did I do?"

"Excellent! Later I will explain how CECO worked its way to the top of my prospect list. I wouldn't have made these transactions on just any stock. But for now let's focus on the naked put as part of the money tree concept."

"Again it is very different from the traditional buy and hold strategy. In fact with naked puts I may never own the stock. Of course it has to be a stock that I would be willing to own because the put might be assigned. But again the concept is to take short term gains on a continuous basis on stocks that I own (covered calls) or stocks that I would be willing to own (naked puts). I pick some cash off the money tree for my CA$H for LIFE account and move on. There are always more trees with more fruit.

"Notice in this example that most of the premiums are for very short periods of time to expiration. I got $.25 per share with only eleven days to expiration. Then I got $.80 per share for thirty-two days to expiration. On August 22, 2005 I got $1.30 per share for 4 months to expiration. Each one of these premiums provides a discount to the purchase of the stock if you are assigned. The farther out you go the larger the premium."

"I see," Jake exclaimed. "*Time is money!* So, what is the desired premium for a naked put?"

"First let me clarify what I just said about discount. Let's say a stock is currently selling for $21 and I sell a $20 put on that stock for premium of $1.00. My discount on that stock is $2.00. That's my security. The stock will have to go down more than $2.00 before I lose money on the transaction.

"Now concerning an acceptable put, my goal on naked puts is to get a premium that is 2 to 10% of the stock price for the shortest time frame possible. That premium represents a discount on the price of the stock in the event I am "put" (have to buy) the stock.

"Here are the guidelines when considering naked put opportunities. The elements that may affect the possible outcome are:

- Time factor—how long to expiration based on the chosen strike month
- The premium to be earned
- The total discount—premium plus difference between stock price and strike price
- The current stock price.

"The premium is dependent on the strike price in relation to the current stock price, the time factor, volatility of the stock and who knows what else. The put premium, just like call premiums, is determined by the dynamics of the market.

Keep in mind I always select a strike price lower than the current market price. That way if I am put the stock I am getting it at a discount from the current price. That discount plus the premium provides my down-side security on the transaction. The greater the current stock price exceeds the strike price the lower the premium and the less the risk. Naturally the premium and the risk are directly related.

"We want to combine these factors in a formula in a way that provides good opportunities but also guides us away from doing the wrong thing. With this in mind use the following to calculate a Put Factor for your prospects."

$$\text{Put Factor} = \frac{6 \,(100 \text{ PR})\,(\text{CP-SP})}{(\text{ME})\,(\text{SP})\,(\text{SP})}$$

Where:

ME = Months to Expiration
PR = Put Option Premium
CP = Current Stock Price
SP = Strike Price

"I have had excellent success with naked puts for stocks when this factor is positive and close to one."

"You will notice that when looking at put options the farther you go out in time at a particular strike price the higher the put option premium and therefore the larger the discount (but also the higher the risk). It is very difficult to predict what can happen as the time element gets longer so be careful with the strike price at which you are willing to buy the stock.

"Whenever I get put option quotes with my VISIONS software, Put Factor is provided, along with all the other important stock and option information to help in the selection process.

"Here is an example of a quote on CECO that shows what I am looking at when I make my naked put selection."

```
Put Options for CAREER EDUCATION [CECO] On 01/11/06 9:04 PM  Price < BL & 50DAvg TAI=Time to Act  _ |□| x|
Print   Throw Away
Put Options for CAREER EDUCATION [CECO] On 01/11/06 Price < BL & 50DAvg TAI=Time to Act
Price 32.06 (-0.65) 52WkHi 42.43 52WkLow 28.73 50DayAvg 34.27 BL 32.15 BR .26 Beta .11

                              Put   Option                                    Mths           Price
Option   Strike   Strike    Premium         Open      Put    Percent  Till  Best    If
Symbol   Date     Price    Bid   Asked   Interest  Factor  Discount   Exp   Fit  Assigned
------   ------   ------   ----- -----   --------  ------  --------   ----  ----  --------
CUYMF  1/20/06   30.00   0.15  0.25    10,650   0.62    0.50    <1         29.85
CUYNE  2/17/06   25.00   0.20  0.30       425   1.07    0.80     1    **   24.80
CUYNF  2/17/06   30.00   1.10  1.25     2,499   1.19    3.67     1    **   28.90
CUYPW  4/21/06   17.50   0.05  0.15       160   0.42    0.29     3         17.45
CUYPD  4/21/06   20.00   0.15  0.25     1,205   0.81    0.75     3    *    19.85
CUYPX  4/21/06   22.50   0.30  0.40       732   1.01    1.33     3    **   22.20
CUYPE  4/21/06   25.00   0.60  0.75     6,340   1.21    2.40     3    **   24.40
CUYPF  4/21/06   30.00   1.90  2.05     5,045   0.78    6.33     3    *    28.10
CUYSW  7/21/06   17.50   0.15  0.25       109   0.67    0.86     6         17.35
CUYSD  7/21/06   20.00   0.35  0.45        70   0.99    1.75     6    *    19.65
CUYSX  7/21/06   22.50   0.60  0.75       728   1.06    2.67     6    **   21.90
CUYSE  7/21/06   25.00   1.10  1.20     1,287   1.16    4.40     6    **   23.90
CUYSF  7/21/06   30.00   2.55  2.70     1,029   0.55    8.50     6         27.45
```

"Here is a summary of the put factor for all the CECO trades."

Put Factors for CECO					
Date	Stock Price	Strike Price	Option Premium	Months to Expiration	Put Factor
12/06/04	39.86	30.00	0.25	0.37	4.44
12/20/04	36.98	30.00	0.80	1.07	3.48
01/06/05	40.32	30.00	0.50	1.43	2.41
02/09/05	40.21	35.00	0.90	1.23	1.87
02/14/05	39.60	35.00	0.65	0.13	11.27
06/06/05	35.45	25.00	0.75	4.57	1.65
06/13/05	38.99	30.00	0.75	1.07	4.20
07/11/05	38.79	30.00	0.35	1.30	1.58
07/15/05	40.60	35.00	0.70	1.17	1.64
08/22/05	37.76	30.00	1.30	5.03	1.34
11/08/05	35.12	25.00	1.05	5.47	1.86

"Be very cautious if the put factor is less than one. If it is negative you have selected a strike price that is greater than the current stock price. Make sure this is what you want to do since your chances of assignment are much greater even though it might still be at a discount if the premium is high enough.

"You mentioned there must be a catch. There is an investment needed to accomplish a naked put trade even though it is not shown on the chart. Since these are naked puts you need sufficient cash or margin in your brokerage account to make these trades. The amount varies by brokerage firm. My broker requires a cash or margin reserve of 20% of the put purchase price plus the premiums received. If this is a cash reserve it is earning interest at the broker margin rate so in a sense one could be double dipping—earning premiums and interest!"

"One of my most successful strategies has been what I call *The Double Up*. Let's say you like a certain stock and would like to invest in it over time, but you are a little concerned about current trend and momentum. That stock is a prime candidate for the *Double Up*. I buy 50% of the desired investment now and sell a covered call with strike price close to the market price. I also sell an equal number of naked puts at a strike price lower than the current market price. At this point there will be three possible results:

"**Stock Price Down** in which case the puts are assigned, the calls will expire and I now have my intended investment and continue to sell covered calls."

"**Stock Price Close To Unchanged** in which case the puts and calls both expire. This is where I started except I have pocketed nice premiums for selling the puts and calls. And I'm ready to repeat the process, again selling covered calls and naked puts, picking more money off the money tree."

"**Stock Price Up** in which case the calls are assigned and the puts expire. In this case I am back to a total cash position with respect to this investment with a significant gain. At this point I would go back to my prospect list and consider new candidates for another *Double Up* or one of my other strategies.

"Here's an example that illustrates my *Double Up* strategy. The company is SanDisk (SNDK), one of the leading providers of memory cards that are used in portable devices like your digital camera and Blackberry. They had just reported record earnings when I started this sequence."

Rob slid the SanDisk chart across the table.

SANDISK CORP					SNDK SWQ JAN APR JUL OCT			
01-10-05	B		1000		24.13	24135.00	-24135.00	
01-10-05	S	10	FEB	22.50	2.75	2729.95	-21405.05	CA
01-10-05	S	10	FEB	20.00	.40	379.98	-21025.07	PE
02-18-05	C		1000		22.50	22480.25	1455.18	<

"I decided that an investment of 2000 shares would be in order. So using my *Double Up* strategy on January 10 I bought 1000 shares at $24.13 and sold February calls with a $22.50 strike price. I earned $2,729.95 on the transaction. These are called In-The-Money (ITM) calls since the strike price is smaller then the current stock price. The stock market was in a downward trend in early January 2005. I did this to provide myself with some downside protection. Because of the premium earned SNDK could go down to $21.38 from where I bought it before I would lose money on this investment. I also sold 10 contracts of February puts with a strike price of $20."

"My cautious approach was effective. The 1000 shares on which I had sold calls were purchased for $22.50 and the put contracts I had sold expired. "

"I earned $1,455.18 in 39 days. I had $22,480.25 invested for a gain of 6.47%."

"Hold on professor. I've got a question."

"Sure. Go ahead."

"I need to be sure I understand, what did you call it, 'In the Money'. Oh yes, I remember, that's selling a call with a strike price less than the market price. Part of the premium you might have to give back if the call is assigned. And that's what happened here. You actually earned less than the premiums. I computed some of those in my homework assignment. But what I want to know is why you decided on an In-the-Money option?"

"Good question Jake. The reason is that I was anticipating a downward drift in the market. I wanted downside protection because . . ."

"But wait a minute professor. What do you mean you anticipated a downward shift?"

"Jake, you've asked a very important question and a very big question. I'm currently working on a book to answer that specific question. All stock investors would like to know which way the market is moving. For right now let me just say that all large universities, research analysts at major brokerage houses and of course the Federal Reserve Bank have economists who develop elaborate formulas to model the market.

"I have also developed a market simulator which I call The Money Tree Stock Market Simulator. Try a free demo from my website, **RonGroenke.com**. You might want to experiment with it. But for right now let's stay focused on puts.

"Would you like to see a few more examples of *Double Up?*"

Under his breath Jake was muttering, "Focus, focus, (simulate the market?), focus, focus. "Oh, yes professor. One step at a time. Let's get back to puts."

"Here are two more interesting companies," Rob said as he looked through his folder. "They demonstrate how you can improve the return on a covered call strategy by selling a naked put also. The first is EGL Inc. which provides air and ocean freight forwarding. Here I did an At-The-Money (ATM) call and a naked put.

"Jake you should be pretty good at reading these charts now."

EGL INC			EAGL	KUF	FEB	MAY	AUG	NOV	
06-20-05	B		900			20.22	18203.00	-18203.00	
06-20-05	S	9	NOV	20.00	2.20		1959.96	-16243.04	CA
06-20-05	S	6	NOV	17.50	.85		494.98	-15748.06	PE
11-18-05	C		900			20.00	17980.40	2232.34	<

"Yes I think so. Let's see. You bought 900 shares, sold a covered call at strike price of $20.00 and then a naked put at a $17.50 strike price. Apparently the stock price was above $20.00 at expiration day, 3rd Friday in November, because you ended with all cash. A nifty little profit of $2,232.34 or 12.42% in just five months."

"Right, and it's interesting to me if you break down the profit into two parts," Rob replied. "If I had done only covered calls the profit would have been $1,737.36 or 9.66%. Decent enough but the puts boosted the profit by $494.98 adding almost 3% to my gain.

"Here is another *Double Up* investment in Cree Inc. a semiconductor materials and devices company.

"Again my profits were enhanced by adding puts to the basic covered call strategy."

CREE INC					CREE CQR	MAR	JUN	SEP	DEC
02-18-05	B		1100			23.20	25525.00	-25525.00	
02-18-05	S	11	JUN	22.50	2.80	3059.95	-22465.05		CA
02-18-05	S	10	JUN	17.50	.35	329.98	-22135.07		PE
06-17-05	C		1100			22.50	24730.17	2595.10	<

"There is one more variation that I use. Before I get to that Jake, would you summarize what we've covered so far?"

"Sure," Jake replied looking quickly at his notes. "We started off with . . . I guess you would call it a pure naked put. With Career Education you sold numerous puts and they all expired. By the way how would you compute your return on that?"

Rob smiled, shrugged his shoulders and said, "Some say infinity since the investment was zero. Or is it to infinity and beyond?"

Jake looked over his notes again and continued. "So the first one is the pure naked put where all your puts expire and you never actually own the stock. And the second one is the Double Up where you buy half of your intended investment and sell puts for the other half. And you say there is one more. Hmmm. Could it be a case where you intend to have a pure naked put but you have to buy the stock?"

"Very good," Rob congratulated his former and now once again student. "Always, when I sell a put, it is on a stock that I would not mind buying, especially at the discounted strike price. So I know that's a possibility. And since it is a stock I am willing to buy it is one I am willing to sell a covered call on. Here is an example of my put to covered call strategy."

SIGMATEL					SGTL	UGO	MAR JUN	SEP DEC	
08-22-05	S	17	DEC	15.00	.70	1169.96	1169.96	PA
10-24-05	S	4	DEC	12.50	.50	184.99	1354.95	PE
12-16-05	B		1700		15.00	25519.00	-24164.05	
12-19-05	S	17	MAR	15.00	1.00	1682.22	-22481.83	CO
03-17-06	P		1700		15.00	25480.15	2998.32	<

"On August 22 my analysis indicated that Sigmatel (SGTL) had moved through its low point and was in a twenty day up trend. I sold December $15.00 naked puts, 17 contracts four months out. In October I sold 4 December $12.50 contracts two months out since I had some additional margin available in my account."

"I was almost right. The price dipped below $15 just in time for me to have the $15 put assigned. The $12.50 put expired. I then sold a covered call three months out on the 1700 shares I was required to buy."

"I can hardly wait to get started," Jake exclaimed, rubbing his hands together. "Do you make more money on puts or calls? It looks like maybe puts are more profitable."

"No Jake, don't jump to that conclusion. I know investors who have done nothing but sell puts and they've gotten clobbered. There is more risk involved with naked puts than with covered calls. If we hit a serious bear market a put seller can be devastated.

"I've been very successful and I would have to say that one key has been that I have combined a generally optimistic view of the overall market with as much risk avoidance as reasonably possible.

"Limit yourself to 40% or less of your account value that you have tied up supporting naked puts. Look at this as a way to preplan some of your new investments for some of your covered calls which may be assigned. You might as well buy stocks at a discount if you can."

"If you are assigned a stock at expiration you can always sell it the next trading day if you feel things have changed such that you do not want to own the company."

"This is exactly what I did with an assignment of General Motors (GM) stock on December 16, 2005."

Here is the data on GM:

GENERAL MOTORS						GM	GM JAN	APR JUL OCT	
03-23-05	S	40	SEP	15.00	.55	2134.92	2134.92		PE
03-29-05	S	10	MAY	25.00	.65	629.97	2764.89		PE
05-26-05	S	10	JUL	27.50	.40	379.98	3144.87		PE
06-06-05	S	10	JUN	30.00	.55	529.97	3674.84		PE
11-18-05	S	30	JUN	10.00	1.10	3272.36	6947.20		PO
11-21-05	S	10	DEC	22.50	.80	784.96	7732.16		PA
11-21-05	S	20	DEC	17.50	.12	219.98	7952.14		PE
12-06-05	S	40	MAR	7.50	.40	1564.92	9517.06		PO
12-16-05	B		1000		22.50	22519.00	-13001.94		
12-19-05	S		1000		22.16	22154.91	9152.97		<

"Remember in early 2005, GM came out with guidance that indicated they were going to have negative earnings. On the first big drop in the stock I waited a few weeks and after the price stabilized at about 28, I felt a September 15 put was safe. I received $.55 per share and was willing to buy 4000 shares at $15.00 and had the account margin to cover it."

"GM did recover somewhat after Kirk Kerkorian made a huge investment at $31.00 a share. The September $15.00 puts therefore expired worthless."

"Then when the stock went down again (low of 21.19 on November 16, 2005) I saw the opportunity to sell additional puts."

"The stock was down in late December and I was put 1000 shares at $22.50 on Friday, December 16. To be safe I immediately sold these on the following Monday at $22.16 and still came out with a small gain of $420.87 (22154.91 + 784.96 − 22519.00) on the transaction."

"You must be ready to buy a stock when a put is assigned but you can also take action (sell in this case) to reduce potential risk."

"One could also sell only naked puts against an all cash account. The strategy here is you would only begin to own any stocks through the assignment of a put. All of your stock purchases are then at a discount. Again you would only do this with companies you would like to own but at a lower price.

"Here is a summary of the type of action one may take depending on individual stock and overall market trend."

"Sell In-The-Money (ITM) covered calls if there is concern that the stock may go down. The more one is In-the-Money the greater the downside protection one has but at the cost of a lower gain. Remember Insurance does cost money. This is a good strategy for short-term gains that beat money market or CD rates.

"Sell At-The-Money (ATM) covered calls if it appears that the stock (or market) is flat and going nowhere. The downside protection is the premium received. The gain can be excellent if done over and over."

"Sell Out-of-The-Money (OTM) covered calls when a stock is in a good up trend and the overall market is rising (rising tide lifts all boats). The gain is not only the premium received (some downside protection) but also from stock appreciation. The stock appreciation is received only if the stock is called. If a stock does not go up far enough to be called you get the *If Expired* gain. Gain from appreciation is not experienced until you sell at a higher price. The gain here can be significant."

"Sell Out-of-The-Money (OTM) Naked Puts on good stocks at a strike price below the buy limit. You need cash or margin in your account to cover a possible assignment. Do this on stocks that you are considering for covered calls. Buy half now, sell a covered call and also sell an equal number of naked puts at a strike price below the buy limit (Double Up strategy). This concept can enhance the gain by a number of percentage points over a straight covered call. I will explain what I mean by buy limit later.""

"Okay professor I'm ready. I can't wait to get started. This seems too good to be true but what can be the catch."

Rob smiled as he looked at his student and thought to himself, *my friend you are not even close to being ready.* To Jake he said, "Actually there is a catch."

Jake's face dropped. "But professor you've shown me it works and you are making Ca$h for Life with the money tree strategy. What do you mean about a catch?"

"Jake, suppose you were ready to get started, what is the first thing you would do?"

"I guess I would start off slow with just the covered call strategy. I would learn that first before going to naked puts. Right?"

"Right," Rob agreed. "And what is the first thing you would need to do?"

"Buy a stock."

"Which stock?"

After a moment, just a bit dejectedly, "Oh."

"We've still got much work to do. Thursday after Rotary I will begin explaining my stock selection strategy."

"I'll get the bill," said Jake.

"Let's not forget a good tip for Tiffany."

6

Build the Prospect List

Apply yourself; get all the education you can, but then . . . do something. Don't just stand there, make it happen.
Lee Iacocca

The Rotary Club meeting had ended and Jake had waited patiently as Rob met the Membership Chairman and filled out the paperwork to be proposed for membership. Tiffany again seated them at a secluded table in a spacious area of the restaurant. Because Jake was tall, she knew he needed plenty of room. After seating them she brought each a cup of herbal tea.

Rob noticed how diligently Jake was going over his notes as he waited and commented, "I seem to recall that you made an A in my Finance 101 course."

Jake laughed. "No not exactly professor. I had an A going into the final. But then I got distracted toward the end of the semester. Her name is Katie. I would like for you to meet her. We've been blessed with three daughters and five grandkids."

"That's wonderful. Jean and I enjoy our kids and grandkids too. But let's get back to business. I've got two questions for you. First, do you understand the money tree concept?

"I think so," Jake responded as he gathered his thoughts. "To me it's a rather radical concept for investing. Different from all my traditional understanding. We had a speaker at the Forum Club in Naples recently. A guy named John Bogle. He made a lot of sense. His strategy seems to be to invest in an index fund, keep transaction costs low and ride the market up over the long term. Last week Katie and I had Tiffany and her boy friend over for lunch. Nice guy I guess, but really not good enough for Tiff. Anyway she was telling about the investing philosophy of her investment club. If I remember correctly . . ."

"I heard that!" Tiffany had good ears and was just coming around the corner.

Winking at Rob, "He's never liked any of my boy friends. Cut me some slack Jakey. A girl's got to have a little fun."

"Jake was telling me about the philosophy of your investment club. Could you explain it," Rob asked.

"Sure. We are members of **NAIC**, National Association of Investors Corporation. They provide a lot of support, monthly magazine and such. There are four basic principles. Make regular investments, reinvest all earnings and dividends, invest in growth equities, and diversify. But like I said earlier the concept of options has never come up. Why do you think that is?"

"My guess," Rob responded "is they are not familiar with how conservative and risk free a covered call transaction is. Like most people when they think of options trading they are thinking of buying rather than selling. But actually my strategy would be perfect for an investment club. I've worked out a rational process of stock selection and ranking. And having done it both ways, I much prefer the money tree concept. By the way Jake was just explaining his understanding of the concept. Can you join us?"

"No, I've got to get back to the front. But how about giving a presentation to our investment club?"

"Be glad to. Set it up and let me know." And she was off. "Okay Jake, tell me about the money tree concept. That's my first of two questions for you."

"Obviously it's entirely different from the traditional investing that you hear from John Bogle or learn in investment clubs. The key there is stock appreciation over time. With the money tree concept you are more interested in how much fruit you can pick off the tree rather than how tall the tree may grow. In the case of calls you are happy if your stock gets bought. And in the case of puts you may never even own the stock. I see definite advantages. You have short term relationships with stocks so you are not likely to get emotionally involved. And you get paid up front when you sell a call or put. That money is yours no matter what. Oh and one other thing. You make money even in a stagnant market. And perhaps even in a down market like that investment you showed me in **IDCC**. You don't need stock appreciation to make money. That's about it. How did I do?"

"Very good. I think you've got it. Now here's your second question. What does the money tree concept have in common with investment clubs?"

Jake was surprised at the question. He finally understood how different the two concepts were. How could they have any thing in common?

"Gee professor, I'm drawing a blank. They seem to be entirely opposite." Glancing over his notes he suddenly saw the answer.

"Oh, I've got it. It's what you said we would cover next after the money tree concept. Building a qualified prospect list and ranking the stocks. I understand that's also the main topic of discussion in investment club meetings, the merits of various stock candidates for investing. Am I right?"

"Absolutely. The most important decision before selling a call or put is stock selection." Rob glanced at his watch. "I'm meeting Jean in 30 minutes. Let's talk about building a qualified prospect list and then we will cover ranking the stocks later.

"Remember, at this point we are simply building a qualified prospect list and organizing it into marketplace or technology areas with three or four companies in each area. We are like the owner of a major league baseball team. We want a lot of players on the farm team. And of course we want to develop player-prospects for each position. But just because a stock makes it onto the prospect list does not mean we are about to buy it. Many farm league players never make it to the big league. Using my software program we easily sort the list to determine our best prospects. I also continue to include on the prospect list stocks I have bought or on which I've sold a naked put. I continue to include them in the ranking process to be sure they are still viable.

"There is no limit to how many stocks you can have on your prospect list. But each stock you include must pass the following seven tests:

    1) An options market must exist for the stock.
    2) Annual sales or revenue of at least $250 million per year ($500 million is desirable).
    3) Market Cap of $500 million or more ($750 million is desirable).
    4) Positive revenue growth (10-15% per year is desirable).

5) Positive earnings for three of the last four quarters (positive for the last four quarters is desirable).

6) Positive Bare Cash ($100 million or more is desirable). Bare Cash is cash plus marketable securities less long term debt.

7) Average daily trading volume of at least 250,000 shares per day (500,000 shares per day is desirable).

"You have to search for good companies since they are not obvious. You should first look in an industry or market that you are familiar with. No matter what your background is, you probably can name thirty to fifty companies very quickly that touched your life in the last twenty-four hours one way or another. From the cereal you had for breakfast, the type of vehicle you drive, the brand of gas you use, the last store you shopped, to the computer on your desk, there are various companies that could have filled your needs. You picked certain ones because of a fuzzy feeling for the product or good advertising on the company's part. I like the computer and communications networking business. I therefore have a prospect list that is weighted heavily in the computer systems, software, networking, and semiconductor markets. I have supplemented this list with companies in the retail, defense, medical technology, and air transportation areas.

"Identify several marketplace or technology areas that you like and understand. There are a number of places to find these candidates. You could research the Dow 30 members, look at all 500 stocks in the S&P 500, or search the entire market. My software actually lets you search the entire market, some 8,000 stocks, and display the ones that meet your criteria for market cap, PE, sales revenue, etc. That usually results in a list of about 1,000 stocks which are candidates for further analysis with VISIONS."

"I always consider stocks that are in the highest volume of shares traded for the day as prospects. High volume is important for two reasons. First you want to always have a market for your stocks. High volume indicates high liquidity. Second, high volume indicates that the market has scrutinized the company very closely. When the market focuses intently on a company, all information available is reflected in the price of the stock. You can then conclude that the stock is accurately priced by the market. No hidden surprises are likely. Look also at the percent gainers and losers list for the day. Check the news. Why did a particular stock go up or down so much in one day? Maybe an analyst upgraded or downgraded the stock, the company beat or missed their earnings estimate, there is new competition, there is a take over rumor or the rumor has been dispelled, etc. There are many reasons. Sometimes something major has happened . In many cases it is temporary and this may be an opportunity worth tracking. "

"I also have found many prospects by looking at the major markets' daily and weekly new low lists. Every company has a 52-week high and low. Stocks do go up and down. When good companies hit a new low this is the time to place them on your prospect list and start tracking them. At some point they will move up from this new low and that may be the time we want to get in. We want to buy low and sell calls as the stock moves up. All of this information is available in the *Wall Street Journal* and *Investors Business Daily* or on various web sites like Yahoo Finance and Market Watch."

Rob pulled a sheet of paper out of his notebook and handed it to Jake. "Here's a list of thirty stocks on my prospect list which I have arranged in ten groups of three. This is just an example. Actually I have over 100 stocks that I track as prospects. You will need to form your own list based on your particular interests and field of expertise."

ROB GRAHAM PROSPECT LIST	
WalMart (WMT)	Oracle (ORCL)
Costco (COST)	Microsoft(MSFT)
Target (TGT)	Symantec (SYMC)
Imclone (IMCL)	Sandisk (SNDK)
Pfizer (PFE)	Seagate Technology (STX)
Merck (MRK)	Western Digital (WDC)
Agilent Tech (A)	Cisco Systems (CSCO)
Cree Inc (CREE)	Extreme Networks (EXTR)
Citrix Systems (CTXS)	Foundry Networks (FDRY)
Lockheed Martin (LMT)	Sun Micro (SUNW)
General Dynamics (GD)	Hewlett Packard (HWP)
Honeywell (HON)	Dell Computers (DELL)
JetBlue Airways (JBLU)	Cardinal Health (CAH)
Southwest Airlines (LUV)	Boston Scientific (BSX)
AirTran (AAI)	Medtronic (MDT)

Jake had written down the seven tests for stocks to pass before being included on his prospect list. "Professor concerning the data for the tests, how do I get that information?"

"No problem. The information is readily available on numerous web sites. For example **www.yahoo.com** or **www.marketwatch.com**. My search engine software, **VISIONS**, uses these and other websites to find quality stocks and what I call the diamonds. Those are the calls and puts that meet my criteria."

Rob's cell phone rang just as Tiffany rounded the corner with an excited expression. "Yes Jean, I'm leaving in two minutes. Love you.

"Professor," Tiffany exclaimed. "I just talked to the president of our investment club. We had a cancellation and our planned guest speaker can not come tonight. Could you fill in?"

7

Buy Low—Sell High

Create your own vision of happiness.
Jean Groenke

The investment club met at the home of its president, Nicholas Gardner, a past president of Rotary and active citizen of Marco Island.

Tiffany introduced Rob and Jake to Nicholas and wife, Kris, as the members mingled and enjoyed Kris's punch and cookies. The beautiful home was at the end of a street, typical of Marco Island, with a wide canal on each side and bay to the front. The house was surrounded on three sides with water and was designed to take full advantage of the views.

Jake and Tiffany took their seats. Nicholas, having a flair for introductions because of his exceptional voice, called the meeting to order.

"Tonight," he began, "we are pleased to have a retired finance professor and new resident of Marco Island as our speaker. Please give your attention to Dr. Rob Graham."

There was friendly applause as Rob stood beside the flip chart facing the group of investors.

"Thank you Nicholas and members and especially Tiffany for inviting me tonight. It's always a pleasure to share investment information with interested, intelligent investors. I'm somewhat familiar with NAIC. I admire your dedication to periodic investing and your diligent analysis of individual stocks. As you know there are many very complicated and sophisticated methods of stock analysis. Over the course of my teaching career I've explored the intricacies of fundamental analysis and technical analysis. Each has its pros and cons. But in the final analysis what it all comes down to is that old cliché: Buy Low—Sell High."

Rob continued. "When you look at the history of each stock in

45

your portfolio you see that each was purchased at some point in a cycle which has now become evident. The full nature of the cycle was not evident at time of purchase. Hind sight is 20:20. We can look back and see that some were bought at a low point in the cycle and then moved up. Some were bought at a high point in the cycle and then moved down. Those in the later group may have now moved back up. Over time your gain is greatest in those stocks which you bought at the low point of their cycles.

"Now the question I asked myself, 'Is there anyway to increase the odds that I am buying at the low point of the cycle?' Take the two extremes. At the end of each trading day there are stocks which have closed at a 52 week high. And there are also stocks that closed at a 52 week low. Assuming you have eliminated consideration of stocks with low liquidity, negative earnings or declining sales, which stocks are most likely to be at the bottom of their cycle?

"I offer no guaranties but I have personally been very successful with stocks moving up from their 52 week low.

"The formulas I will give you are to compute what I call Buy Limit and Buy Rank. These two values allow me very quickly to filter my prospect list and rank the stocks. For every stock you can get its lowest price of the past 52 weeks and its highest price. Let L stand for the 52 week low and H stand for the 52 week high. The Buy Limit formula is as follows." Rob wrote the following formula on the flip chart.

$$\text{Buy Limit} = L + .25(H - L)$$

"Ideally we would like to buy at L, the 52 week low. But we have to accept the fact that we cannot time the market and know that today's L will not be superseded by an even lower L tomorrow. But it is possible we can catch the stock on the way up from L. That's our objective here. The critical increment is .25(H - L). For example if a stock has a 52 week low of $10 and a 52 week high of $40 then the critical increment is $7.50. That's computed by taking 25% of $40 minus $10. You might think of 7.50 as our window of opportunity. I would be interested in buying the stock in the price range from $10 to $17.50. As we get closer to $17.50, the *Buy Limit*, I begin losing interest in the stock. At $17.50 it is too high. It's easy to see the trend when you are looking at a chart of the stock's prices. I'll show you one in just a moment.

46

"Now we use the Buy Limit in the following formula to compute the Buy Rank for each stock. Let's let BL stand for Buy Limit and CP stand for the Current Price of the stock. Notice that the denominator is the critical increment we computed to use in the last formula.

$$\text{Buy Rank} = \frac{10(BL - CP)}{.25(H - L)}$$

"When the current stock price is the same as the 52 week low the buy rank is 10. This is its maximum value. When the current stock price is the same as the 52 week high, the buy rank is negative 30. Our Buy Rank formula gives us a range of values on a scale from negative 30 to positive 10."

Rob drew the following on the flip chart below the two formulas.

"A stock captures my attention with a Buy Rank between 10 and 5, moving down. A decreasing value in the Buy Rank indicates the stock is moving up in price and perhaps has started its next major up trend. Also note that positive is good and negative is bad.

"For example using our example of a stock with 52 week low of $10 and 52 week high of $40, we computed the Buy Limit to be $17.50. Suppose the current price were $12. At that price we are well below our Buy Limit of $17.50. What is the Buy Rank? It is 10(17.50 - 12) which is 55 divided by 7.50. That's a Buy Rank of 7.33. As the current price rises closer to the Buy Limit, the Buy Rank declines, approaching zero. For example a current price of $16 gives a Buy Rank of 2. A current price of $17 gives a Buy Rank of 0.66. And of course a current price of $17.50, the same as the Buy Limit, would give a Buy Rank of zero. So we are only interested in stocks with a positive Buy Rank. The VISIONS software computes the Buy Limit and Buy Rank of each stock on my prospect list. Then by clicking on the Buy Rank title in the sort and filter panel box my prospect list is sorted from best to worse.

"Are there any questions?"

Nicholas stood up, rubbing his chin and still looking at the simple formulas. "Rob," he said "this reminds me of Tiger Woods playing golf.

He makes it look easy. With mastery comes ease of application and explanation. Does anyone have any comments or questions for Rob?"

"Did you originate these formulas," someone asked.

"Yes. I haven't seen them anywhere else," Rob replied. "When I started building my prospect list I began intuitively looking at the list each day of stocks trading at their 52 week low. Frequently the stock would be down because of a bit of sensational news and the market had over reacted. If the fundamentals were good I would add that stock to my prospect list. Also it seemed obvious to me that the greatest potential losses would come from stocks trading at 52 week highs."

A murmur went through the group as various members mentioned stocks that had resulted in losses.

"Oops," said Rob. "Did I hit a nerve?"

With a rueful smile Nicholas commented, "Our group got excited about Symantec last fall. We had lots of discussions and analysis. Lots of Wall Street analysts had a buy recommendation on the stock. Finally in November of 2004 we bought in at about $30 a share. It's been a downhill slide since."

"That's interesting," Rob replied. "Symantec is a stock that I've had success with. I followed my Buy Limit and Buy Rank rules and did very well. I like the company. It is a world leader in Internet security technology. It provides a broad range of content and network security solutions to individuals and enterprises. Would you like to take a look at my investment strategy with Symantec?"

All were interested in any way they could avoid their recent debacle. Rob had noticed a large screen high definition TV behind the flip chart. "Nicholas, do you mind if I use your TV screen? I can show you my investment in Symantec."

Nicholas quickly turned the TV on and removed the flip chart. Rob punched commands into his **PDA**.

"Symantec (**SYMC**) has been on my prospect list since 2003. To do our analysis we need some pertinent information about the stock. There are many places on the internet that provide this information for free. One favorite is **www.marketwatch.com**. Enter a stock symbol and then go to "Profile." Here's the key information for November 4, 2004 when the club made their investment."

The following information was displayed on the TV screen.

SYMC stock price $30.03
52-week high - $31.10
52-week low - $14.85
50 day average stock price - $26.96
Revenue of over $2 billion per year.
Market Cap of over $15 billion.
Sales growth of 38% for the year.
Earnings were positive the past eight quarters.
Bare Cash of over $2 billion.
Average number of shares traded per day of over ten million
shares.

Rob continued, "The fundamentals are very good and pass my seven tests. So far so good. Here's the Buy Limit and Buy Rank calculation with my Buy Limit, Buy Rank Wizard."

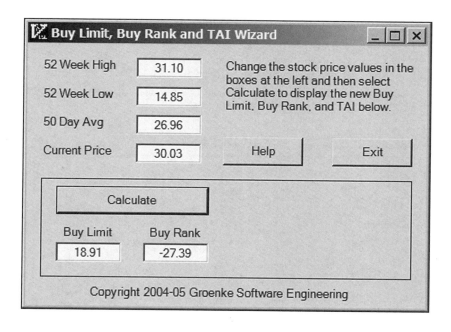

"The Buy Rank is −27.39 which indicates to me that it is a bad idea right at this time. The stock is trading near its 52 week high and that could be a problem if the market goes down, there is a downgrade of the stock, or some negative news."

"Now let's take a look at when I made my move with SYMC. Let's move the calendar forward six months to May 24, 2005."

Here is the data:

> SYMC stock price $22.13
> 52-week high - $33.48
> 52-week low - $18.23
> 50 day average stock price - $20.24

"Using these values in the Wizard we get a Buy Limit of 22.03 and a Buy Rank of -.27.

"Everything looks good at this point. Before finally making the investment I also check to see where the stock is trading in relation to its fifty-day moving average. I like to get the very best odds I can," Rob explained. "I've found that it's not enough to have a stock with a good Buy Rank and good return for selling calls. Those are both critically important. But I want to be as sure as possible that the stock has actually started another up trend. So before investing I look at a picture of the stock. Here is where a picture could be worth thousands of dol-

lars. I want to see the current price pass through the fifty day moving average. As long as the current price is leading the average down, don't invest. This is what was happening after the big drop in December until the turn up in early May.

"When the price breaks above the fifty day moving average, I feel encouraged that we have begun an up trend. Does that make sense?" (See figure at bottom of previous page.)

"Finally on May 24, 2005 with the stock trading above the 50 day average I did the following." Rob punched on his PDA.

SYMANTEC CORP					SYMC	SYQ	JAN	APR	JUL	OCT
05-24-05	B		1000		22.11	22115.00	-22115.00	
05-24-05	S	10	OCT	22.50	1.90	1879.93	-20235.07	CA
10-21-05	C		1000		22.50	22480.25	2245.18	<

"I bought 1000 shares at $22.11 and sold OTM (Out-of-The-Money) covered calls five months out with a $22.50 strike price. The $2,245.18 I received is a 10.15% return for five months on the $22,115 investment." Rob paused to let this information sink in with the investment club.

For a few moments the group was silent as the members considered the powerful concept of "Buy Limit" and "Buy Rank." All had taken notes and written down the formulas.

Seeing their note taking Rob commented, "Don't forget that my VISIONS software will do all the work for you. For all the stocks that the club is considering VISIONS will compute the Buy Rank and Buy Limit and you can sort either column. VISIONS will also allow you to sort the list based on just fundamental analysis as Bare Cash, Shares Traded, Positive Earnings for Last Four Quarters, Market Cap, Beta, PE and other factors that you choose."

Tiffany was the first to ask a question. "Professor, I'm really impressed. Your stock analysis seems to be both simple and powerful. However I'm really interested in making money by selling options. Would you explain covered calls? I'm not sure I understand exactly what happened in the chart you had on the screen."

"Thanks for the question Tiffany. Yes, a key reason I bought SYMC, in addition to its good fundamentals and Buy Rank, was that it had good call option premiums. Before buying the 1000 shares I looked at several different options possibilities. I like to sell options with a strike price slightly above or at the purchase price which in this case is $22.50. I looked at the premiums for expiration dates in July and October. The returns are different for "If Sold" and "If Expired." If the option expires I only earn the option premium. But if the stock is called, meaning it's sold, I earn the premium plus a small amount of capital gain.

"Here are the call options when the price of the stock was at $21.88:"

Call Options for SYMANTEC CP [SYMC] On 05/24/05					
Price 21.88 52WkHi 33.48 52WkLow 18.23 50DayAvg 20.24 BuyLimit 22.03 BuyRank .39					
		Call Option Premium		% Gain if Sold	% Gain if Expired
Strike Date	Strike Price	Bid	Asked		
07/15/05	20.00	2.30	2.50	1.92	10.51
07/15/05	22.50	0.65	0.75	5.80	2.97
10/21/05	20.00	2.80	3.00	4.20	12.80
10/21/05	22.50	1.80	2.00	11.06	8.23

"On the day I did the analysis the market was offering to pay me $.65 a share for the option to buy my shares at a price of $22.50 up to the third Friday in July, about two months later. I could have received $1.80 a share for an October expiration. The longer the expiration period the more money I could make. I opted to take the five month profit.

"You see," Rob continued, "my investment strategy involves a concept I call the money tree. Rather than being strictly interested in stock appreciation I pick money off the money tree on a continuous basis by selling options."

Looking at Nicholas, Rob asked "Has the investment club ever considered selling options?"

"No," Nicholas replied, "and I'm not sure why. I have a general impression that options are very risky. But I don't see anything scary about what you just showed us with Symantec."

"Right," Rob agreed. "The value of the money tree approach can be seen by contrasting my investment in Symantec with the standard 'buy and hold' strategy. Here's another picture."

"My stock was called in October 2005. At this point it was trading above the 50 day average and had a Buy Limit of $22.04 and a Buy Rank of −4.28. This Buy Rank says one should wait. "

"By imposing the Buy Limit and Buy Rank restraint on myself I avoided buying Symantec at any time other than the low point in its cycle. Symantec had a negative Buy Rank in October of 2005. So I shifted to other stocks in my prospect list which have a positive Buy Rank.

"A good idea since in early November 2005 a number of analysts downgraded the stock and it lost over $4.00 per share. It continued down for almost two months and then started to turn positive in January 2006. It is now again in the area where one needs to be ready to do a covered call or naked put as it moves up through the 50 day average and establishes a new up trend."

One of the club members, had pulled his chair up closer to the TV and was intently analyzing the Symantec investment. "Professor, I've got a question."

"Yes sir. Fire away," Rob responded.

"Because you sold those call options in May 2005, you were forced to sell 1000 shares of Symantec at $22.50. Consequently you missed the big run up to over $24 just a few weeks later."

"Yes, that's true," Rob agreed. "I missed the opportunity to sell at the high point. But how many investors actually do that. Most would continue holding the stock expecting it to go even higher. Not selling the call is better only if you would have sold at that high. How often is that done?

"Which would you say is more rewarding? Is it better to have the thrill of the ride up and down or is it better to steadily pick money off the money tree by selling options? That's a decision for each investor to make."

There was chatter from the club members as they began discussing the merits of selling options. For most it was a brand new concept. Nicholas stood up to regain control of the meeting. "Rob, you've certainly given us a challenging presentation. This is a strategy we need to discuss. But just one final question so I'm sure I understand. You apparently make money in the stock market by selling options. Are you not interested in market appreciation?"

Rob thought for a few seconds searching for the right words to explain his strategy. "I am interested in market appreciation but not for the same reason as most investors. Your club for example spent a lot of time analyzing investment options and then settled on Symantec at $30. You tried to pick a stock that was going up over the long run. And eventually you may be right. Although you might note that investors who bought RCA at its high point in the 1920's have still not recovered their investment.

"Basically I think you set yourself a very difficult task when you try to pick market winners. The very best stock analysts are seldom right more than 50% of the time. Look at how few mutual funds out perform index funds. And none out perform index funds on a consistent basis.

"But having said that, I am careful about stock selection. I require a positive Buy Rank based on the formulas I showed you. That is a very stringent requirement that has served me well, although certainly not perfect. I've been burned several times with what I thought were good companies. However any loss that I incurred because the stock went down was cushioned by the premiums I garnered by selling calls.

"There are basically two reasons I am very careful with stock selection. And these are not the typical reasons you would hear from the average investor or market analyst. Most investors, like this investment club, are trying to buy the right stocks for price appreciation. Frankly, as I said, I think that's just too difficult for anyone to do on a consistent long term basis. The two reasons I want stocks likely to go up are: 1) Avoid losses and 2) The option premiums are higher if the market has positive expectations for the stock. My return on selling options is so good that I don't really need stock appreciation. What I'm doing with my stock selection strategy is playing good defense as I consistently pick money off the money tree.

"Here is an example of an investment in Boston Scientific (BSX) that I made in June 2005. They are one of the leading providers of stents and other medical devices that are used in interventional medical specialties."

Rob punched BSX on his PDA and the following information was displayed on the TV screen.

BSX stock price $28.91
52-week high - $42.80
52-week low - $27.09
50 day average stock price - $29.03
Revenue of over $6 Billion per year.
Market Cap of over $20 billion.
Sales growth of 2% for the year.
Earnings were positive the past four quarters.
Bare Cash of over $500 million.
Average number of shares traded per day of over four million shares.
Buy Limit $31.01
Buy Rank of 5.35

"A good opportunity that meets my criteria and starting to move up from a new low at the end of May 2005."

I reviewed the following chart and decided an investment at this time was appropriate."

Rob punched on his **PDA** again and the following trade data was displayed. "You might be interested in another example showing how I analyze each of my investments.

BOSTON SCIENTIFIC CORP						BSX	BSX FEB	MAY AUG	
06-15-05	B		1000			28.70	28705.00	-28705.00	
06-15-05	S	10	NOV	27.50	3.10	3079.95	-25625.05		CE
06-15-05	S	10	AUG	25.00	.40	379.98	-25245.07		PE
11-21-05	S	10	JAN	27.50	.65	634.97	-24610.09		CO
01-21-06	P		1000			27.50	27480.08	2869.98	<

"On June 15, 2005 I bought 1000 shares of BSX at $28.70 and sold 10 Nov 27.50 **ITM** (In-The-Money) calls for $3.10 netting $3079.95. I sold **ITM** calls because I wanted to give myself some downside protection just in case **BSX** again turned down. I also decided that an August naked put at a strike price of $25.00 would be okay since the new low was $27.09. This naked put at $25.00 was also over $6.00 below the Buy Limit at this time."

"Well here I was wrong. No one can bat 1000. Two months after my move, **BSX** started down again and set a new low in November. My naked put expired in August and my call expired in November but I still had a gain of $3459.93 (3079.95 + 379.98) on this investment during this time. The call and put option sellers lost all this money. My strategy of selling an ITM in June was right on. I could have sold the stock at this point for $26.26 for a gain of $1009 on this investment. I however felt that BSX is a good prospect and therefore sold a covered call again at a strike price of $27.50 two months out for $.65. The idea here is to wait for BSX to move higher and then either get called out at $27.50 or sell more calls every few months to generate income in my CA$H for LIFE account.

"My first goal with any investment is to have a positive cash flow. My second goal is to have a *very* positive cash flow. When I make an investment I am buying something so that is cash out. I show that as a negative balance in the last column. As I make money with the investment by selling options or having stock called, that's cash inflow which eventually gives me a positive balance in the last column. The S in a row indicates the sale of an option. At the end of that row you can see the type and disposition of the option sale. For example the sale on June 15, 2005 was a call option which expired (CE). 'Expired' means the option on expiration day was worthless. The same for sale of the naked put on June 15. PE indicates that put option expired worthless. The CO on the November 21, 2005 sale indicates that this call is still open. If the stock gets called this becomes a CA (call assigned). 'Assigned' means my 1000 shares were purchased by the option holder, in this case for $27.50 per share. The cash inflow will be $27480.08 as shown in the last row. If this happens, the total gain will be $2869.98."

Nicholas walked over to Rob and held out his hand. "Thank you so much for your presentation. I'm sure our club will benefit. Our track record is actually pretty good despite having bought a few stocks at the wrong time. I can definitely see the value of your formulas.

"By the way did you say you have software that is useful in analyzing stocks and finding good calls and puts?"

"Yes that's true. I call my stock and options search engine VISIONS. You are welcome to download a free trial from my website (**RonGroenke.com**).

"I've enjoyed the evening. Perhaps I should leave you with one cautionary note."

8

A Note of Caution

*You should invest in companies that even a fool
can run, because someday a fool will.*
Warren Buffett

"**I** want to emphasize," Rob continued, "that no stock market system is full proof. You have all been impressed with the return available by selling options.

"But there is always the clear and present danger that the stocks you have selected can go down and totally wipe out any profit you've made from selling options.

"A prime example of what can happen in the real world is the trade experience I had with ValuJet (**VJET**). You already guessed it. I owned the stock when one of their planes crashed. Lets review what happened.

"On 05-03-96 I purchased 2000 shares of **VJET** for \$13.50 each and sold December 12.50 calls for a premium of \$3.375. A gain of 25% if expired and 19% if called out in seven months. On May 11, 1996 a ValuJet DC9 crashed into the Everglades in Florida with no survivors. The price of the stock was affected when all of ValuJets planes were grounded. Since I had losses built into my plan I took action on 06-18-96 and closed out my call options (bought them back) and sold the stock the next day. This is noted in line two of the table as **CC** for Closed Call.

"What started out to be a good trade turned into a sizable loss with zero warning. Tragic and unforeseen events will happen when least expected. Have some built into your plan.

"I do everything I can to protect against stock market surprises. In fact I have losses built into my plan. I'll tell more about that later.

"I keep this account summary with me as constant reminder of what can happen."

The following chart flashed on the TV screen.

VALUE JET					VJET	VJQ MAR JUN	SEP DEC	
05-22-96	B		2000		13.500	27029.00	-27029.00	
05-22-96	S	20	DEC	12.50	3.375	6664.77	-20364.23	CC
06-18-96	B	20	DEC	12.50	.750	1550.00	-21914.23	
06-19-96	S		2000		6.625	13221.00	-8693.23	<

9

Jake's Prospect List

Invest in companies, not stocks
Peter Lynch

The next morning Jake hurried out to purchase a copy of Investors Business Daily. As they left the investment club meeting the night before Rob had suggested he build a qualified prospect list of at least 15 companies, which met the criteria for sales, earnings and liquidity. For each company he was to compute the Buy Limit and Buy Rank.

After last night's session with the investment club, Jake was more motivated than ever to learn everything he could about the professor's options strategy. He knew the professor had a lot more to teach him, but he also knew the importance of getting the basics down. So he very dutifully went about his homework assignment, building a qualified prospect list. Flipping through the Investors Business Daily he began listing companies that he recognized. Soon he had over 50 companies. Next he grouped the companies into market place or technology areas. In some cases he was not sure what category to place the company. He went to google.com and checked the company's website to be sure. While on the internet he did a search for pharmaceutical companies and discovered a list of 213 companies. To keep his analysis manageable he decided to limit his list to five categories and find three qualified candidates in each category. He had a variety of categories including retail electronics stores, computer chips, pharmaceuticals, book stores, and computer makers.

Going through his notes he found the seven tests that each company must pass before it could be on his prospect list. He decided to make a spreadsheet listing his potential prospects down the left side of the page the seven tests across the top. These were

1) An options market must exist for the stock.

2) Annual sales or revenue of at least $250 million per year ($500 million is desirable).

3) Market Cap of $500 million or more ($750 million is desirable).

4) Positive revenue growth (10-15% per year is desirable).

5) Positive earnings for three of the last four quarters (positive for the last four quarters is desirable).

6) Positive Bare Cash ($100 million or more is desirable). Bare Cash is cash plus marketable securities less long term debt.

7) Average daily trading volume of at least 250,000 shares per day (500,000 shares per day is desirable).

The professor had recommended several internet sites for company financial information. Looking through his notes Jake found three:

www.yahoo.com
www.moneycentral.msn.com
www.marketwatch.com

As he was about to start the long process of surfing the web to get the financial information for each company, the phone rang.

With his mind still on the daunting task of searching for the data he slowly picked up the phone.

"Hello."

"Jake, this is Rob Graham."

"Professor, good morning. I'm just working on my prospect list."

"I thought you might be. Have you started to search for the data on your prospects and begun computing Buy Limit and Buy Rank?"

"I was about to but I am getting a headache just thinking about all the surfing and computations."

"Not a problem," Rob assured him. "Just go to my website. **RonGroenke.com**, and download my VISIONS software. Then you will be able to easily get all the data and the Buy Limit and Buy Rank for all your prospects with the click of your mouse."

Jake downloaded the software and entered the list of companies and started the search engine. Jake's headache immediately began to ease. A few minutes later the table was complete with Buy Limit and Buy Rank scores from the following formulas.

$$\text{Buy Limit} = L + .25(H - L)$$

$$\text{Buy Rank} = \frac{10(BL\text{-}CP)}{.25(H - L)}$$

As Jake became familiar with the software program he discovered that he could easily sort and filter the whole list by any column. He selected positive Revenue Growth and the last four quarters of positive earnings . Then he selected **DO** to filter the list.

"Katie, could you come take a look at this." They were usually within speaking distance of each other.

As Katie looked over his shoulder at the computer screen Jake explained his prospect list.

"These are fifteen stocks that we might buy. I'm analyzing each stock based on its current financial data." Jake showed Katie the list and how he could Do and UnDo the filtering of the list."

"Now here is another trick I can do with the professor's software." Jake clicked on the Buy Rank heading in the filter panel box. The list was automatically rearranged so that the Buy Rank column was sorted from most positive to most negative value."

Jake started explaining Buy Limit and Buy Rank. "The Buy Limit is the maximum price we would pay for a stock. When you see that the Last Price exceeds the Buy Limit then the stock is already too high. Our objective is to buy low and the buy limit keeps us on the low end."

Katie recognized one of the stocks. "I see you have Radio Shack on the list. How good is a Buy Rank of 7.20.

"Very good. Notice that the Buy Limit is 24.03. and the current price is $21.52. $24.03 is the most we would be willing to pay for Radio Shack at this time."

"Oh," Katie said with a big smile. "That's great. You know we have

From your VISIONS Storage Bin. Jake's Prospect List **************** 01-10-06 10-47 PM** ▢✕

Print Now Report Save Data Save Symbols Throw Away Set/Show Filters UnDo Sort Help Best Fit Key Help/Definitions Web Links BL/BR Wizard Ready

Company Name	Stock Symbol	Search Date	Quote	52Wk High	52Wk Low	50Day Avg	Buy Limit	Buy Rank	TA/I	Best Fit Beta	P/E	Div Yld%	?	Opn Vol/Day	Mkt Cap	Bare Cash	Rev/Year	% Rev Gth/Y	Qtrly Erngs
CAREER EDUCATI	CECO	01-04-06	32.43	42.43	28.73	34.69	32.15	-0.82	TA ***	0.11	15.0	0	Y	1M	3B	331M	2B	14.1	++++
CHECK POINT SO	CHKP	01-04-06	21.28	25.38	19.57	21.22	21.02	-1.80	TA **	2.50	17.6	0	Y	2M	5B	954M	566M	9.1	++++
COGNOS INC	COGN	01-04-06	34.32	47.40	31.56	34.12	35.51	3.00	TA **	1.87	23.7	0	Y	1M	3B	522M	880M	0.9	++++
CISCO SYS INC	CSCO	01-04-06	17.85	20.25	16.83	17.42	17.68	-1.99	TA **	2.22	20.7	0	Y	53M	109B	6B	25B	9.7	++++
DELL INC	DELL	01-04-06	30.76	41.99	28.62	30.96	31.96	3.59	TA ***	1.22	23.8	0	Y	22M	72B	9B	54B	11.3	++++
WALT DISNEY-DI	DIS	01-04-06	23.99	29.99	22.89	24.92	24.66	3.77	TA	1.17	19.6	1.1	Y	8M	46B	-7B	31B	2.5	++++
ENZON PHARM IN	ENZN	01-04-06	7.48	13.83	5.70	7.17	7.73	1.23	TA	1.23	N/A	0	Y	468K	331M	189M	169M	8.9	++++
HUTCHINSON TEC	HTCH	01-04-06	29.46	43.00	23.78	27.35	28.58	-1.84	TA	0.95	15.7	0	Y	527K	753M	206M	631M	29.4	++++
INVESTORS FIN	IFIN	01-04-06	37.56	53.44	30.64	38.24	36.34	-2.15	TA ***	1.33	16.4	0.2	Y	718K	2B	5B	665M	13.7	++++
JUNIPER NETWOR	JNPR	01-04-06	21.36	27.65	19.65	22.73	21.65	1.44	TA ****	3.65	40.0	0	Y	7M	12B	1B	1B	45.7	++++
LUCENT TECH IN	LU	01-04-06	2.72	3.86	2.35	2.79	2.72	0.00	TA	3.21	11.2	0	Y	43M	12B	-627M	9B	1.2	++++
POLYCOM INC	PLCM	01-04-06	16.02	23.20	13.97	15.84	16.27	1.08	TA **	3.11	25.8	0	Y	1M	1B	214M	571M	2.6	++++
QLOGIC CP	QLGC	01-04-06	31.52	43.66	28.20	32.49	32.06	-1.04	TA ***	3.54	17.3	0	Y	1M	2B	812M	605M	16.4	++++
RADIOSHACK COR	RSH	01-04-06	21.52	34.48	20.55	22.52	24.03	7.20	GR	1.13	9.6	1.2	Y	1M	2B	-69M	5B	8.5	++++
VERISIGN INC	VRSN	01-04-06	21.10	33.36	19.01	22.62	22.59	4.15	TA ****	3.49	22.5	0	Y	4M	5B	737M	1B	27.5	++++

Visions Stock Filters [X]

A B C D E F   Get   A   Set   Do   UnDo

Set these filters to the criteria for your search.   Set All to Any

Stock Symbols	Stock Price	Buy Rank (†)	P/E Ratio	TAI (†)	Div Yield	Best Fit (†)	Beta
Any ▸	Any ▸	Any ▸	Any ▸	>WT ▸	Any ▸	Any ▸	Any ▸

Options Req'd	Share Vol/Day	Rev/Year	Market Cap	Rev Growth/Yr	Bare Cash	Qtrly Earnings
Any ▸	Any ▸	Any ▸	Any ▸	> 0 ▸	Any ▸	All 4 of 4 + ▸

Select Favorite then Get to retrieve filter template.

Select Favorite, enter name, then set to save template.

From your VISIONS Storage Bin. Jake's Prospect List ************* 01-10-06 10-47 PM**

Print Now Report Save Data Save Symbols Throw Away Set/Show Filters UnDo Sort Help Best Fit Key Help/Definitions Web Links BL/BR Wizard Ready

Company Name	Stock Symbl	Search Date	Quote	52Wk High	52Wk Low	50Day Avg	Buy Limit	Buy Rank	TA I	Best Fit	Beta	P/B	Div Yld%	Opn ?	Vol/ Day	Mkt Cap	Bare Cash Year	Rev/ Cash Year	% Rev Gth/Y	Qtrly Erngs
RADIOSHACK COR	RSH	01-04-06	21.52	34.48	20.55	22.52	24.03	7.20	GR		1.13	9.6	1.2	Y	1M	2B	-69M	5B	8.5	++++
VERISIGN INC	VRSN	01-04-06	21.10	33.36	19.01	22.62	22.59	4.15	TA	****	3.49	22.5	0	Y	4M	5B	737M	1B	27.5	++++
WALT DISNEY-DI	DIS	01-04-06	23.99	29.99	22.89	24.92	24.66	3.77	TA		1.17	19.6	1.1	Y	8M	46B	-7B	31B	2.5	++++
DELL INC	DELL	01-04-06	30.76	41.99	28.62	30.96	31.96	3.59	TA	***	1.22	23.8	0	Y	22M	72B	9B	54B	11.3	++++
COGNOS INC	COGN	01-04-06	34.32	47.40	31.56	34.12	35.51	3.00	TA	**	1.87	23.7	0	Y	1M	3B	522M	880M	0.9	++++
JUNIPER NETWOR	JNPR	01-04-06	21.36	27.65	19.65	22.73	21.65	1.44	TA	****	3.65	40.0	0	Y	7M	12B	1B	1B	45.7	++++
ENZON PHARM IN	ENZN	01-04-06	7.48	13.83	5.70	7.17	7.73	1.23	TA		1.23	N/A	0	Y	468K	331M	189M	169M	8.9	++++
POLYCOM INC	PLCM	01-04-06	16.02	23.20	13.97	15.84	16.27	1.08	TA	**	3.11	25.8	0	Y	1M	1B	214M	571M	2.6	++++
LUCENT TECH IN	LU	01-04-06	2.72	3.86	2.35	2.79	2.72	0.00	TA		3.21	11.2	0	Y	43M	12B	-627M	9B	1.2	++++
CAREER EDUCATI	CECO	01-04-06	32.43	42.43	28.73	34.69	32.15	-0.82	TA	***	0.11	15.0	0	Y	1M	3B	331M	2B	14.1	++++
QLOGIC CP	QLGC	01-04-06	32.46	43.66	28.20	32.49	32.06	-1.04	TA	***	3.54	17.3	0	Y	1M	2B	812M	605M	16.4	++++
CHECK POINT SO	CHKP	01-04-06	21.28	25.38	19.57	21.22	21.02	-1.80	TA	**	2.50	17.6	0	Y	2M	5B	954M	566M	9.1	++++
HUTCHINSON TEC	HTCH	01-04-06	29.46	43.00	23.78	27.35	28.58	-1.84	TA		0.95	15.7	0	Y	527K	753M	206M	631M	29.4	++++
CISCO SYS INC	CSCO	01-04-06	17.85	20.25	16.83	17.42	17.68	-1.99	TA	**	2.22	20.7	0	Y	53M	109B	6B	25B	9.7	++++
INVESTORS FIN	IFIN	01-04-06	37.56	53.44	30.64	38.24	36.34	-2.15	TA	***	1.33	16.4	0.2	Y	718K	2B	5B	665M	13.7	++++

Visions Stock Filters [X]

Set these filters to the criteria for your search.

A B C D E F | Get

Select Favorite then Get to retrieve filter template.

Select Favorite, enter name, then set to save template.

Stock Symbols [Any] [A] Do UnDo Set All to Any | Set

Stock Price	Buy Rank (1)	TAI (1)	Best Fit (1)	Beta
Any	Any	>WT	Any	Any

P/E Ratio	Div Yield	Options Req'd	Share Vol/Day	Market Cap	Bare Cash
Any	Any	Any	Any	Any	Any

Rev/Year	Rev Growth/Yr	Qtrly Earnings
Any	>0	All 4 of 4 +

Copyright 2004 Groenke Software Engineering

2000 shares of Radio Shack I inherited from Aunt Candace. Wonder how much we could make selling calls on those 2000 shares?"

"That's right," Jake replied. "I had forgotten about that stock. We should look at selling calls on this stock since it is sitting in our account and not doing much. I'll use VISIONS to search for some call options on Radio Shack while you fix us a cup of coffee."

Jake started the call options search engine and entered RSH for call options on Radio Shack. In a few seconds a table (see next page) appeared.

"Radio Shack closed today at $22.02. Lets consider that as our purchase price since we inherited the stock we don't really have any investment cost in it. For tax purposes if we were to sell we would have the cost basis used in the estate tax return but I don't know what that is right now."

"Wait a minute. Let me be sure I understand this." Katie tapped the 4/21/06 22.50 row. "What's a 1.20 bid mean?" Before Jake could answer she asked, "What is 2000 times $1.20?" Jake smiled as he did the computation. Sometimes his wife surprised him with her quick insights.

"The answer is $2,400. That's the amount we could receive by selling calls on our 2000 shares of Radio Shack. Today is January 10, 2006. April options will expire on April 21, 2006, that's the 3rd Friday in April."

Katie followed the April 21 line across to 7.63 and 5.45. "Does this mean that the return for selling the calls will be either 7.63% or 5.45%? Why is there a difference?"

The question hearkened back to Jake's first homework assignment. He wrote down the two formulas and began explaining the difference.

If Sold =	$\dfrac{\text{(Strike Price + Premium − Purchase Price)}}{\text{Purchase Price}}$
If Expired =	$\dfrac{\text{Premium}}{\text{Purchase Price}}$

"Only one of two things will happen and in either case we get to keep the $2,400." Jake noticed that Katie was looking at the kitchen.

Call Options for RADIOSHACK CORP [RSH] On 01/11/06 11:11 AM Price < BL & 50DayAvg TAI=Get Ready

Print   Throw Away

Call Options for RADIOSHACK CORP [RSH] On 01/11/06 11:11 AM Price < BL & 50DayAvg TAI=Get Ready
Price 22.02 (-0.02) 52WkHi 34.48 52WkLow 20.55 50DayAvg 22.38 BuyLimit 24.03 BuyRank 5.77 Beta 1.12

Option Symbol	Strike Date	Strike Price	Call Option Premium Bid	Asked	Open Intrst	% Gain If Sold	Gain If Exprd	*Magic Chart* % If Sold	% If Exprd	Mths Till Exp	Best Fit	Break Even Price	Down Side (%)	Bid/StkPr (%)
RSHAX	1/20/06	22.50	0.35	0.40	3,287	3.77	1.59	2.27	1.80	<1	***	21.67	1.59	1.56
RSHBX	2/17/06	22.50	0.75	0.80	626	5.59	3.41	6.80	5.40	1	*	21.27	3.41	3.33
RSHDD	4/21/06	20.00	2.70	2.85	1,621	3.09	12.26	10.00	8.00	3	*	19.32	12.26	13.50
RSHDX	4/21/06	22.50	1.20	1.30	1,313	7.63	5.45	10.00	8.00	3	*	20.82	5.45	5.33
RSHDE	4/21/06	25.00	0.40	0.50	684	15.35	1.82	10.00	8.00	3	*	21.62	1.82	1.60
RSHGW	7/21/06	17.50	5.10	5.30	200	2.63	23.16	14.80	11.90	6	*	16.92	23.16	29.14
RSHGD	7/21/06	20.00	3.20	3.40	54	5.36	14.53	14.80	11.90	6	*	18.82	14.53	16.00
RSHGX	7/21/06	22.50	1.80	1.90	326	10.35	8.17	14.80	11.90	6		20.22	8.17	8.00
RSHGE	7/21/06	25.00	0.85	0.95	520	17.39	3.86	14.80	11.90	6	*	21.17	3.86	3.40
VJYAW	1/19/07	17.50	5.70	5.90	19	5.36	25.89	24.40	19.70	12	*	16.32	25.89	32.57
VJYAD	1/19/07	20.00	3.90	4.20	513	8.54	17.71	24.40	19.70	12	*	18.12	17.71	19.50
VJYAE	1/19/07	25.00	1.55	1.70	1,457	20.57	7.04	24.40	19.70	12	*	20.47	7.04	6.20
VJYAF	1/19/07	30.00	0.45	0.65	5,792	38.28	2.04	24.40	19.70	12	*	21.57	2.04	1.50

She had recently mentioned some remodeling plans if only they had the extra money. "Uh, Katie, you were asking about the difference between 7.63% or 5.45%. Look I'll show you. See the two formulas. To compute the gain if the call expires, meaning the stock is not called by the option holder because the market price is $22.50 or less on April 21, simply divide the premium by the purchase price. That would be $1.20 divided by $22.02." Jake showed her the answer of 5.44959.

"Let's compute the gain "If Sold" for the April 22.50 calls. That would happen if the stock price is above $22.50 on April 21. Using the other formula it would be $22.50 plus $1.20 minus $22.02 divided by $22.02." Using his calculator Jake showed Katie the answer of 7.63%.

"Okay," Katie said, "I see the difference. If the stock is called you have to take into account the difference between the strike price and the purchase price. Since the strike price is a little more than the purchase price we make more if the stock is called."

"That's right," Jake replied. "You've got it." Jake took a bite of a cinnamon roll and puzzled over the table. "But what I don't understand is which option should we sell. The July 22.50 option would give us a return of over 10% for just a few months more. April expirations are just a little over three months away from today." He was concentrating so hard on the Radio Shack analysis he didn't hear Katie leave to answer the phone. She soon came bustling back with a big grin.

"Jake you are not going to believe who was on the phone.

Rob and Jean Graham have just invited us over to their condo for lunch tomorrow. They have someone they want us to meet."

10

What's the Best Option—
The Magic Chart

Success is the progressive realization of a worthy goal.
Earl Nightingale

Riding up the glass elevator to the Graham's penthouse condo, Katie and Jake had a panoramic view of Marco Island. On their left was the Yacht Club at the foot of the Jolley Bridge, which connected the island to the mainland of southwest Florida. They saw a small jet which had taken off from the Naples Airport, about 20 miles to the north. The owner apparently wanted a view of Marco before making a sharp turn to the north. On their right they could see all the way to Goodland, a small community also on the island with another bridge connecting to the mainland. The elevator was for the exclusive use of the two penthouse condos at the top of the most recent luxury tower built on the beach. As they stepped out onto the open foyer they had views of the beautiful crescent beach to the north and the south.

"I wonder who they want us to meet," said Katie as Jake pushed the door bell. Before the melodic chime had ended Jean Graham opened the door and warmly welcomed them in.

"Come in," she smiled. "We are so glad you could come over. I've heard about you, Jake, from my husband. And Katie, what a beautiful sundress! Did you get it here on the island? Jake, Rob is on the balcony. Why don't you go on out. There's a glass of ice tea waiting for you out there. We'll join you in a moment." Jean had the graceful movements of a ballerina as she motioned Jake in the direction of the balcony.

Jake left the two women to get acquainted as he walked across the wide expanse of the Great Room. The view outside was magnificent but he was mainly intrigued by the wide collection of paintings and artifacts. He quickly noticed items from the Orient, Australia and Europe. *World travelers*, he decided.

As he stepped out onto the balcony he had the commanding view of the gulf to the west. The noon sun was just high enough to begin casting its rays on the west balcony. Rob called from the corner to the north. "Come around here Jake. We can have the shade and still enjoy the view."

As Jake took a comfortable seat and noticed that Rob was reading "The World is Flat" by Tom Friedman. Setting the book aside Rob commented, "We've always been so rushed in our prior meetings. Maybe this afternoon we can have a good visit. I've wanted to ask you about your book. You mentioned that you sold your CPA firm and moved to Marco to write a novel."

Mention of the CPA firm brought back many mixed emotions for Jake. There was the satisfaction of serving his clients and the frustration of having to jump through so many senseless—and sometimes contradictory—hoops. *Like a trained show dog*, he thought.

"Yes, well, I seem to have writer's block here lately. The novel idea comes from my work experience. After graduation from the University of Minnesota, I worked for a small accounting firm while preparing to pass the test to be a Certified Public Accountant. The company I was working for had experienced accountants who specialized in auditing, small business "write-up" work and management advisory services. It just so happened that they were weak in the area of tax planning. That was the void that I filled. I was soon the tax specialist. When I started my own firm I continued on in the tax field.

"Just about every year there would be major changes in the tax law. At CPE classes, that's continuing professional education classes, these new tax laws were jokingly referred to as 'The Accountants and Tax Lawyers Relief Act'. That always rankled me. The thought that I was somehow receiving a government subsidy. And then I had to agree that I was indeed receiving a subsidy. The whole tax industry, from the simplest tax preparer to the most elaborate scheme for corporate, estate or personal tax avoidance, is a clear example of what's become known as corporate welfare. So unnecessary when we could have a simplified system based on sales or property values."

Looking down at the gulf Jake could see a pelican diving for a fish. *Now that's an honest living*, he thought. *No bureaucracies and no taxes. The pelican keeps what it earns and earns what it keeps.*

"So my novel is based in the world of public accountants and hopefully exposes what I see as serious flaws in the tax system."

"That's interesting," Rob commented. "But it's liable to get you the nick name of 'Don Quixote'. So many different groups have such a vested interest in a complicated tax system that I doubt it could ever be changed. Think how much power congress would be giving up. Just the possibility of a new wrinkle in the tax code forces all major corporations to hire Washington lobbyist and make political contributions to both parties." Rob stood up and looked out at the gulf and down the beach.

"Jake, bring the binoculars over. They are right there by your chair. Looks like a sail boat race is about to begin."

Jake joined Rob at the railing and they took turns looking at the sailboats in fierce competition about half way to the horizon. Looking down the beach they could see sun bathers of all descriptions and swimmers enjoying the surf. Just below them a volley ball game was in progress with six girls playing against six local guys. The girl's team was in training for the summer Olympics and would no doubt handily defeat the local champions.

"You know Jake," Rob said, handing him the binoculars, "when there is so much beauty in the world it's hard to get caught up in crusades to make changes. If there is a drawback to living on Marco maybe that's it. It's so easy to go with the flow and enjoy life. I enjoy focusing on my investments and spending time with Jean. We keep up with the kids and grandkids. What more does a man need in life? Maybe that's why you have writer's block on your novel. Lighten up. Enjoy life."

Jean and Katie joined them with a platter of sandwiches and pitcher of iced tea. "My specialty," said Jean. "Turkey on wheat with provolone cheese, lettuce, tomatoes and mayonnaise. I hope you like them."

Rob embraced Katie with a friendly hug. "So you are the reason my former student here received a B instead of an A in Finance 101. Well Jake, I can certainly understand your predicament." They all laughed, enjoying the conversation along with the food.

As they finished eating the sandwiches Katie was the first to broach the subject of options. "Rob, we've been learning about your investment strategy. Last night when you called, Jake was explaining to me his understanding of the strategy and we were stumped by a particular problem. Do you mind if we ask you a question?'

"Sure. I thought you might have some questions. I will be glad to share what I've learned about the options market. I don't offer any guarantees but it has sure worked for us."

Jake pulled a printout of the Radio Shack options out of his pocket for the 2000 shares of Radio Shack he and Katie owned. He unfolded the paper and handed it to the professor.

"Professor, we have 2000 shares of Radio Shack which we inherited several years back. I used your software to get this list of options when the closing price of Radio Shack was $22.02. We are ready to sell calls on this stock. But how do we figure which of these many possibilities to select?" (See figure next page.)

Rob smiled. "Radio Shack, interesting company. I have used Radio Shack many times the past few years. Seems to go up and down a lot and is at the same price it was three years ago. That has not helped all of the folks that have bought and held but it has been good for generating a steady income. So which option should you select? You need my Magic Chart. Just a moment I'll get you a copy." Rob walked into his office and returned a moment later.

"What is a good premium for a covered call? That question plagued me for the first couple of years I was selling options. This area is mostly science and a little art. Our goal in selling calls is to generate a number of small gains on a continuous basis. If you want a larger premium the time factor will be longer. *Time IS Money*. How do we strike a balance between time and the overall gain? Through experience on simulating multiple option cycles and allowing for losses I have developed the following rate of return table for option premiums. This table is structured by current month and allows you to quickly determine if the rate of return on the option being considered is acceptable. It does not

Call Options for RADIOSHACK CORP [RSH] On 01/11/06 11:11 AM Price < BL & 50DayAvg TAI=Get Ready

Print Throw Away

Call Options for RADIOSHACK CORP [RSH] On 01/11/06 11:11 AM Price < BL & 50DayAvg TAI=Get Ready
Price 22.02 (-0.02) 52WkHi 34.48 52WkLow 20.55 50DayAvg 22.38 BuyLimit 24.03 BuyRank 5.77 Beta 1.12

Option Symbol	Strike Date	Strike Price	Call Option Premium Bid	Asked	Open Intrst	%Gain If Sold	%Gain If Exprd	*Magic Chart* %If Sold	%If Exprd	Mths Till Exp	Best Fit	Break Even Price	Down Side (%)	Bid/StkPr (%)
RSHAX	1/20/06	22.50	0.35	0.40	3,287	3.77	1.59	2.27	1.80	<1	***	21.67	1.59	1.56
RSHBX	2/17/06	22.50	0.75	0.80	626	5.59	3.41	6.80	5.40	1	*	21.27	3.41	3.33
RSHDD	4/21/06	20.00	2.70	2.85	1,621	3.09	12.26	10.00	8.00	3	*	19.32	12.26	13.50
RSHDX	4/21/06	22.50	1.20	1.30	1,313	7.63	5.45	10.00	8.00	3	*	20.82	5.45	5.33
RSHDE	4/21/06	25.00	0.40	0.50	684	15.35	1.82	10.00	8.00	3	*	21.62	1.82	1.60
RSHGW	7/21/06	17.50	5.10	5.30	200	2.63	23.16	14.80	11.90	6	*	16.92	23.16	29.14
RSHGD	7/21/06	20.00	3.20	3.40	54	5.36	14.53	14.80	11.90	6	*	18.82	14.53	16.00
RSHGX	7/21/06	22.50	1.80	1.90	326	10.35	8.17	14.80	11.90	6		20.22	8.17	8.00
RSHGE	7/21/06	25.00	0.85	0.95	520	17.39	3.86	14.80	11.90	6	*	21.17	3.86	3.40
VJYAW	1/19/07	17.50	5.70	5.90	19	5.36	25.89	24.40	19.70	12	*	16.32	25.89	32.57
VJYAD	1/19/07	20.00	3.90	4.20	513	8.54	17.71	24.40	19.70	12	*	18.12	17.71	19.50
VJYAE	1/19/07	25.00	1.55	1.70	1,457	20.57	7.04	24.40	19.70	12	*	20.47	7.04	6.20
VJYAF	1/19/07	30.00	0.45	0.65	5,792	38.28	2.04	24.40	19.70	12	*	21.57	2.04	1.50

consider risk, so picking the right stock is also key. For that—improving our odds of picking the right stock—we use the Buy Limit and Buy Rank computations. This table is strictly for ranking the value of various options on a particular stock. It allows you to quickly rank for example a three month option at one strike price with a six month option at the same or different strike price. The best option to pick is the one that come closest to matching or exceeding the rate on the Magic Chart. It has successfully generated for me an average gain of 25% or more per year over a ten-year period."

Rob handed Jake an index size card with a chart on the front and the back. One side was for the months January through June. The other side had the months July through December.

Jake found the January column on side one. He went down the column to April and then across to the required percentages. Three months out required a return of 10.0 if sold and 8.0 if expired. The corresponding returns for Radio Shack were 7.63 and 5.45. The 7.63 was within 76% of the guide which may be acceptable. Next he looked down the January column to July. For six months out, the chart required a return of 14.8 and 11.9. Now the options available were within 70% of the guide.

"Professor, it looks like our best bet is with a $22.50 strike price because the $25 strike has such a low return for the If Expired case. But I'm still uncertain whether April or July is best for the $22.50 strike."

"Yes, my chart does not always give clear cut answers. It's a guide. Remember that time is money. In this case I would be tempted to take the 5.4 to 7.6% for the April option. Of course July is also tempting because it's nice to get over 10% for six months."

"What if our 2000 shares of Radio Shack get called?" asked Katie. "What if it goes up to $25 or $30 a share and someone else gets the benefit of all that appreciation?"

"That may well happen," Rob responded. "In fact you can certainly expect it to happen on at least some of your calls. But there is no way of knowing in advance which stocks will go up sharply. My strategy, as I mentioned earlier, is *to generate a number of small gains on a continuous basis.*

"Look again at the percentage gain on the April 22.50 contract.

THE MAGIC CHART – SIDE ONE								
MONTHS TO EXP.	IF SOLD	IF EXP.	JAN	FEB	MAR	APR	MAY	JUN
1	6.8	5.4	FEB	MAR	APR	MAY	JUN	JUL
2	8.4	6.7	MAR	APR	MAY	JUN	JUL	AUG
3	10.0	8.0	APR	MAY	JUN	JUL	AUG	SEP
4	11.6	9.3	MAY	JUN	JUL	AUG	SEP	OCT
5	13.4	10.7	JUN	JUL	AUG	SEP	OCT	NOV
6	15.0	12.0	JUL	AUG	SEP	OCT	NOV	DEC
7	16.6	13.3	AUG	SEP	OCT	NOV	DEC	JAN
8	18.4	14.7	SEP	OCT	NOV	DEC	JAN	FEB
9	20.0	16.0	OCT	NOV	DEC	JAN	FEB	MAR

THE MAGIC CHART – SIDE TWO								
MONTHS TO EXP.	IF SOLD	IF EXP.	JUL	AUG	SEP	OCT	NOV	DEC
1	6.8	5.4	AUG	SEP	OCT	NOV	DEC	JAN
2	8.4	6.7	SEP	OCT	NOV	DEC	JAN	FEB
3	10.0	8.0	OCT	NOV	DEC	JAN	FEB	MAR
4	11.6	9.3	NOV	DEC	JAN	FEB	MAR	APR
5	13.4	10.7	DEC	JAN	FEB	MAR	APR	MAY
6	15.0	12.0	JAN	FEB	MAR	APR	MAY	JUN
7	16.6	13.3	FEB	MAR	APR	MAY	JUN	JUL
8	18.4	14.7	MAR	APR	MAY	JUN	JUL	AUG
9	20.0	16.0	APR	MAY	JUN	JUL	AUG	SEP

Now ask yourself a basic question. Do you want to hold the stock without selling a call option on the chance that it may go up, knowing that it could just as easily go down as up? Or do you want to lock in a gain of at least 7.63% for a period of three months? That's better than you could get on a CD for several years. Remember the price has not moved up much in three years."

"To specifically answer your question about what to do if your stock gets called, that's the purpose of having a prospect list. Your cash position is greater by, first, the $2,400 you receive from selling the calls and, second, by the sell of 2000 shares for $22.50 a share. That's a total of $49,800. A stock that has risen sharply may now be above the Buy Limit and not have a satisfactory Buy Rank. If so you would use the money to buy a different stock with a good Buy Rank. Now you have the compounding effect of selling calls on stock purchased with the premium as well as the principle.

"Since it looks like you may be about to make your first foray into the options market, we had better talk about some of the technical terms you will encounter."

"Wait a minute," Jean interjected. "How about a slice of key lime pie for dessert. And I think it's getting a little warm here. Why don't we move inside and be more comfortable."

As they moved inside Katie commented to Jake, "Maybe we can plant our own money tree, starting with those 2000 shares of Radio Shack?"

11

Selling Calls and Puts

*That some should be rich shows that others may become rich,
and hence is just encouragement to industry and enterprise.*

A. Lincoln

As the two couples settled down on luxurious leather couches, Rob proceeded to explain the technical aspects of options trading.

"Options are traded in the financial world the same as stocks on various exchanges such as the Chicago Board Options Exchange (CBOE), American Stock Exchange (AMEX), Philadelphia and Pacific exchanges. Option orders are placed in your brokerage account and executed on an appropriate exchange. Not all stocks have options, so one needs to check availability by asking a stockbroker or accessing a quote service over the Internet such as at **www.yahoo.com** or **www.cboe.com**.

"Buying and selling options is a little different from buying and selling stock. You usually just buy and sell stocks at a desired price. Option orders however require additional specifications such as expiration month, strike price, and intent (open or closing transaction). This information is communicated through the option symbol and specification of the order being placed.

"Stock and Index option symbols are composed of several different components representing the underlying security and information about the specific option contract. The first two or three letters of an option symbol are the option root, followed by the expiration month code, followed by the strike price code. Strike prices can vary depending on such factors as stock splits and sharp price moves etc. NYSE stocks use their stock symbol as their option root. For example John-

76

son & Johnson is JNJ, General Electric GE, Boeing is **BA**, and Wal-Mart is **WMT**. **NASDAQ** stocks use three letter option roots assigned by the exchange. For example the option root for Applied Materials is **ANQ** and for Microsoft is **MSQ**.

"So an Option Symbol is composed of the Option Root, followed by month code, followed by strike price code."

Rob paused, noticing the confused looks from Jake and Katie. Jean broke the awkward silence with a suggestion. "Rob, dear, why don't you use the Illustrator I gave you for your birthday?"

"Good suggestion. Maybe this will help, Jake and Katie." With that he picked up what looked like leather bound book. Opening it he pushed a button and a large painting on the wall nearest them, a beautiful impressionist painting of a family skiing in the Swiss Alps, turned into a clear three foot by five foot screen. As Rob wrote in the Illustrator the information appeared on the screen for all to see.

"Here's the basic notation for expiration month codes," Rob said as he accessed a database. For each month there is one letter of the alphabet to signify a Call and a different letter to signify a Put.

	CALLS	PUTS
January	A	M
February	B	N
March	C	O
April	D	P
May	E	Q
June	F	R
July	G	S
August	H	T
September	I	U
October	J	V
November	K	W
December	L	X

"Then we use the letters again for stock price codes. One letter of the alphabet represents three possible prices. You will quickly get the hang of it."

A	5, 105, 205	N	70, 170, 270
B	10, 110, 210	O	75, 175, 275
C	15, 115, 215	P	80, 180, 280
D	20, 120, 220	Q	85, 185, 285
E	25, 125, 225	R	90, 190, 290
F	30, 130, 230	S	95, 195, 295
G	35, 135, 235	T	100, 200, 300
H	40, 140, 240	U	7.50, 37.50, 67.50
I	45, 145, 245	V	12.50, 42.50, 72.50
J	50, 150, 250	W	17.50, 47.50, 77.50
K	55, 155, 255	X	22.50, 52.50, 82.50
L	60, 160, 260	Y	27.50, 57.50, 87.50
M	65, 165, 265	Z	32.50, 62.50, 92.50

"Notice how this works in the following examples. In the first one, WMTLJ, the WMT stands for Wal-Mart and is the option root, the "L" stands for December Call, and the J indicates a price of 50, 150 or 250, whichever one makes sense relative to the price of Wal-Mart stock. Of course that's 50.

WMTLJ	Wal-Mart December 50 Call
WMTXI	Wal-Mart December 45 Put
INQGZ	Intel July 32.50 Call
INQOF	Intel March 30 Put
MSQIN	Microsoft September 70 Call
MSQXL	Microsoft December 60 Put
RSHDX	Radio Shack April 22.50 Call
RSHPD	Radio Shack April 20.00 Put

"Options quotes can be found in the newspaper or on the Internet. Two sites on the internet that provide quotes are **www.cboe.com** or **www.yahoo.com**."

"This task is relatively easy when using the **VISIONS** option search engine. If you look closely at your Radio Shack **VISIONS** option printout you will see the option symbol provided in the first column along with the strike date and strike price. It also shows you a comparison of the calculated gains to that of the Magic Chart."

Rob paused. "I'll print out a copy of this for you. But don't worry about memorizing it. It will all be second nature after you've done a few trades. Do you want to keep going?"

12

Placing the Trade

*When buying and selling are controlled by legislation, the
first things to be bought and sold are legislators*

P. J. O'Rourke

Jake nodded agreement and Rob continued. "Now before you run
off to place your trade, it might be good to understand how option
orders should be placed."

"When placing option trading orders it is very important to state
exactly what is intended. If a mistake is made and you execute a wrong
trade you may incur a loss to undo it.

"Option orders like stock orders can be placed in your brokerage
account over the phone by calling a trader, over the phone with direct
keypad input, or over the Internet with on line access to your account.
No matter which way you trade the way an order is placed is important.
I'll put on the screen some basic definitions."

As Rob pushed points in the notebook the following items appeared on the screen.

Sell to Open—You are opening a short position for a specific option.
For example this is what you use to write a covered call.

Buy to Close—You are buying back an option you previously sold,
to close out the option. For example this is what you would do if you
did not want your stock to be called. Also, you would want to do this
if you want to sell the stock. Selling the stock without buying back the
call option would leave you in a high risk uncovered position.

Buy to Open—You are opening a long position for a specific option.
For example this is what you do when you are taking a leveraged position by buying the option instead of the stock.

Sell to Close—You are closing a long position for a specific option. For example this is what you do to capture a gain on your leveraged position.

Market order—The order will be executed at the next available bid price. Use this to buy or sell immediately.

Limit order—The order is executed at the limit price or better if possible.

For the day—The order will expire at the end of the trading day.

All or none (AON)—Buy or sell the number of contracts specified. This condition is used to reduce the possibility of trading only one or a small number of contracts in a multiple contract order. Additional orders may increase your overall commission cost.

Good till canceled (GTC)—The order is open until it is canceled. Most brokerage firms will close GTC orders after ninety days.

"Considering what we've learned so far, your order to sell calls on your 2000 shares of Radio Shack stock might be as follows:

"Sell to open, 20 Radio Shack April 22.50 Calls (RSHDX) at a limit of $1.20 for the day, all or none.

"RSH is the root option symbol assigned to Radio Shack options. "D" indicates that it is an April Call. "X" gives us the price of $22.50

"This order would be filled when someone wants to buy 20 Radio Shack April 22.50 Calls for $1.20 or more. If the market has moved down when the order is placed it may not fill. If the market is moving up it could fill at $1.20 or even higher. If it is not filled before the end of the day it expires.

"A future order to close out this position could be as follows:

"Buy to close, 20 Radio Shack April 22.50 Calls (RSHDX) at the market for the day.

"This order would be filled at the next available ask price for the option. Since it is a market order the actual price for each of the 20 contracts may be different. Also it may be only partially filled."

"Professor, why would we want to buy to close an option?" asked Jake.

"This is an example of managing your accounts while you are waiting for the expiration date. A wise old investor was once asked what he thought the stock market would do. His response was: 'It will fluctuate.' And indeed it will. The stock on which you have sold a covered call will fluctuate in value. As the stock fluctuates so does the premium, or price of the call option. For example you expect to receive $1.20 a share for your call options on Radio Shack. In a few days or weeks that same option, RSHDX, may be trading for $.50 or less. If you think the stock is going to come roaring back, bringing the value of the option with it, then you could "buy to close" at the lower price and sell again later at the higher premium. As a general rule I don't micromanage my accounts during the option period. It's contrary to my philosophy. Once I get the cash into my CA$H for LIFE account it makes no sense to try to time the market and chase stocks up or down. I would rather just move on with life."

"I guess you sleep better that way," Jake mused.

"Okay, let's move on to some record keeping checklists I recommend. A disciplined approach is desirable in preparing an option order to prevent mistakes. Here are the steps I go through in preparing a trade:

Write down the trade that you intend to execute.

Get a quote on the stock and intended option. This will validate the option symbol, strike price, and strike month.

Calculate the return on each premium.

Determine if a market or limit order is appropriate.

Set the price on your order and then submit it.

"For example, you have 2000 shares of Radio Shack in your account. You want to place an April covered call option trade and you do not want to have your stock called for less than $22.50 per share. Now you write down the option quotes you need to make a decision.

Radio Shack stock symbol is – RSH

Radio Shack April 22.50 call symbol is – RSHDX

Radio Shack July 22.50 call symbol is – RSHGX

You go to your quote provider (by phone or over the Internet) request the quote for each symbol and write it down."

Then calculate the expected gains with the If Sold and If Expired formulas.

If Sold =	$\frac{\text{(Strike Price + Premium – Purchase Price)}}{\text{Purchase Price}}$
If Expired =	$\frac{\text{Premium}}{\text{Purchase Price}}$

"You look at the Magic Chart table and determine which call option best fits *the money tree* model.

"With the VISIONS Call Option Search Engine this is all done for you." Lets get a current quote on RSH right now."

See the VISIONS call option output for RSH on January 11, 2006 on the next page.

"Since you want the cash now you decide that a limit order at $1.20 should be filled within seconds.

"You write your order as follows:

"Sell 20 RSHDX April 22.50 Calls to open at $1.10 for the day all or none.

"Now place your order and write its confirmation number on your order sheet.

"When your order is filled write out the detail of the order and the net proceeds of the action on your daily-completed order sheet. Save these sheets until you receive your confirmation from your broker. This is a precautionary measure only. If there are errors in the confirmation you need documentation to perform resolution. You will also need your daily trade results sheet to update your trading files and track your overall results.

"After I started trading options it became important to record and track each and every trade. I have done this since day one and now have the history of every trade I made in my blue file. Why a blue file? For every trade you execute you will receive a trade confirmation in the mail from your broker. To keep these together and easily accessible I put them in a blue file folder instead of the standard cream colored ones. This allowed me to find this file very quickly since I was using it more and more each day. I also have a box on the daily order sheets, which gets checked indicating that the blue file was updated.

"In this blue file folder I have a transaction history tracking sheet on which I record my daily transactions such as, stock buys, call option sales, assignments, close outs, etc. I record the date, the transaction, and the net debit or credit for the trade. This is a running list and fills multiple pages for the year. After receiving the confirmation from the broker I use a highlighter and highlight the debit or credit on the tracking sheet to indicate that I received the trade confirmation and the results agree. The confirmations are filed in the order of the

Call Options for RADIOSHACK CORP [RSH] On 01/11/06 9:36 PM Price < BL & 50DayAvg TAI=Get Ready

Print   Throw Away

Call Options for RADIOSHACK CORP [RSH] On 01/11/06 9:36 PM Price < BL & 50DayAvg TAI=Get Ready
Price 21.80 (-0.24) 52WkHi 34.48 52WkLow 20.55 50DayAvg 22.33 BuyLimit 24.03 BuyRank 6.4 Beta 1.12

Option Symbol	Strike Date	Strike Price	Call Option Premium Bid	Asked	Open Intrst	%Gain If Sold	%Gain If Exprd	*Magic Chart* %If Sold	%If Exprd	Mths Till Exp	Best Fit	Break Even Price	Down Side (%)	Bid/ StkPr (%)
RSHAD	1/20/06	20.00	1.85	1.95	1,193	0.23	8.49	2.27	1.80	<1	*	19.95	8.49	9.25
RSHAX	1/20/06	22.50	0.30	0.40	3,287	4.59	1.38	2.27	1.80	<1	***	21.50	1.38	1.33
RSHBD	2/17/06	20.00	2.15	2.25	81	1.61	9.86	6.80	5.40	1	*	19.65	9.86	10.75
RSHBX	2/17/06	22.50	0.65	0.75	626	6.19	2.98	6.80	5.40	1	*	21.15	2.98	2.89
RSHBE	2/17/06	25.00	0.10	0.20	31	15.14	0.46	6.80	5.40	1	*	21.70	0.46	0.40
RSHDD	4/21/06	20.00	2.60	2.70	1,621	3.67	11.93	10.00	8.00	3	*	19.20	11.93	13.00
RSHDX	4/21/06	22.50	1.10	1.25	1,313	8.26	5.05	10.00	8.00	3	*	20.70	5.05	4.89
RSHDE	4/21/06	25.00	0.35	0.45	684	16.28	1.61	10.00	8.00	3	*	21.45	1.61	1.40
RSHGW	7/21/06	17.50	5.00	5.20	200	3.21	22.94	14.80	11.90	6	*	16.80	22.94	28.57
RSHGD	7/21/06	20.00	3.10	3.30	54	5.96	14.22	14.80	11.90	6	*	18.70	14.22	15.50
RSHGX	7/21/06	22.50	1.70	1.85	326	11.01	7.80	14.80	11.90	6		20.10	7.80	7.56
RSHGE	7/21/06	25.00	0.80	0.90	520	18.35	3.67	14.80	11.90	6	*	21.00	3.67	3.20
RSHGF	7/21/06	30.00	0.10	0.20	4	38.07	0.46	14.80	11.90	6	*	21.70	0.46	0.33

tracking sheet. This allows quick access if a reference is required. If a transaction is not highlighted within two weeks, I call the brokerage house and ask for a duplicate confirmation. It may not have been sent or it may have gotten lost in the mail. This process makes sure there is a paper trail for every transaction for tax or other purposes such as stockholder class action lawsuits. In the latter situation, you may be asked to provide copies of all transactions during a certain period to substantiate a possible claim and participate in any settlement. My greatest use of this record was the settlement on litigation regarding the NASDAQ market makers spread price fixing antitrust action. This is where the US Department of Justice brought a civil enforcement proceeding on July 17, 1996, alleging that twenty-four NASDAQ market makers, together with others, conspired to widen spreads in violation of the federal antitrust laws. To participate in this settlement, one had to supply detail records of related NASDAQ stock transactions for the defined period.

"The blue file contains all transactions in the order of execution by date. I also maintain a group of computer files called directory nineteen. In this directory I maintain a file by company of every transaction executed. From this directory I can extract every trade on any company that I have invested in and print out the trading history and corresponding overall gain or loss. I process this directory on a periodic basis to update my successful company list and to track overall results. I use the stock symbol as the file name, which prevents duplication while still being very informative. I backup this directory monthly and keep multiple backups for history and recovery if needed. All of the examples I've shown you are from this history file."

Jake raised his hand to ask a question and then with an embarrassed grin brought it back down. "Professor, I'm convinced this record keeping is important. But at this point I'm lost."

"Hmm, yes I can understand this might be confusing. I developed it as I needed it and have been doing it so long it seems very simple to me. I have an idea," Rob continued. "Why don't I put examples in the software programs that you can download from my website? [RonGroenke.com] That should make your record keeping easy."

There was a buzz from someone downstairs wanting to come up. Jean excused herself.

Rob continued. "One other important record keeping requirement is a tax file. For taxes you need to actually move some cash from your brokerage account to a savings or money market account. This way you are not tempted to invest it. It is reserved for taxes so leave it there. You do not want to have to close out some calls and sell some stock in April to pay the taxes. It could be bad timing. Remember we are reserving for taxes because we plan to make money. It is one of the perks when you have gains. The amount to reserve depends on your tax bracket but here is a good formula:

Tax Reserve = (Total Option Premiums −Losses) x 25%

"Speaking of taxes," Jean said jokingly as she returned with the visitor.

Except for the long hair worn in a ponytail and the diamond stud in his left ear, the man looked like Rob Graham.

Rob rose with a smile and said, "Jake, Katie, I would like to introduce my twin brother, Greg. Greg these are our friends, Jake and Katie Kimball."

As hands were being shook Rob continued. "Greg is a distinguished professor of mathematics. He has been working on a formula that I think you will be interested in."

13

When to Act with a View

There are plenty of good five cent cigars in this country. The trouble is they cost a quarter. What this country needs is a good five cent nickel.

Franklin P. Adams

"Look at these incredible shells I found on Sand Dollar Island. And the birds! I can't get over it. You people actually live here. I'm just now beginning to relax. Soon I'll be back in the frozen north land."

Greg's New England pale skin had taken on a Marco Island tan in the week he had been visiting. Jean brought coffee for everyone and a slice of pie for Greg.

As the group settled back down Rob picked up his leather note pad. "Greg has developed a formula that I believe will be very valuable.

"Jake you know how important it is to pick the right stock. That's where I put my greatest emphasis. First build a qualified prospect list. Then qualify the list with Buy Limit and Buy Rank formulas. And finally you want to be sure the current price has crossed over the fifty day moving average."

"I'm with you up to this point," said Jake. "I've done all the homework although I haven't put it into practice yet."

Rob continued. "There are a lot of times when looking at a stock chart with a fifty-day moving average that I notice that the current price is below the Buy Limit and the fifty-day average. The stock is a prime prospect but the time for action is not quite here. How can I tell when it is time to act? I do not want to be too late but not too early either. I always felt there should be some way to combine the value of the Buy Rank with the fifty day moving average.

"I was inspired one evening when Jean and I were out walking and saw a shooting star, a small meteorite flashing across the earth's atmosphere. Some meteorites are reflected with a flash and others enter the atmosphere and display a burning tail as they near the earth. Why not develop a Take Action Indicator that signals when you should proceed with buying a stock and selling a covered call based on the current price approaching the buy limit and fifty-day moving average. Only when these values begin to converge should buy action be taken. The challenge was putting the information into a formula that would give a reliable and consistent ranking.

"So when Greg came for a visit I knew he would soon be bored without a math challenge."

Greg smiled and sipped his coffee.

"Greg, why don't you explain it from here," said Rob as he handed over the note pad.

"I should explain that, thanks to brother Rob, I have been supplementing my teaching income for the past year with options trading. In the back of my mind was the thought that there should be something more definitive than the Buy Rank for taking action. But I hadn't actually made the conceptual leap until Rob explained the objective.

"There is an ideal situation and then next best. The ideal situation is when the buy rank is greater than five, the fifty-day average is flat or increasing, and the current price has just crossed the fifty day moving average.

"The next best is when the buy rank is positive and the current price is nearing or has just moved above the 50 day moving average. So here's the formula." Greg punched a few buttons on the note pad and the following formula appeared on the screen.

$$TAI = 10 \times \frac{(CP)(CP) + 3(FDA)(BL - CP) - (BL)(CP)}{(CP)(L-BL) + 2(FDA)(BL - L)}$$

Greg continued as if it were the simplest thing in the world. "TAI stands for Take Action Indicator. CP is the current price of the stock that you are considering. FDA is the fifty-day moving average. BL is the Buy Limit and L is the fifty two week low."

With a look of utter despair Jake said, "Greg please. By the time I figure out this formula we'll be at the next expiration date."

"Oh," replied Greg in mock surprise. "Did you want the simple version? Well as a matter of fact I did get it a little simpler. In this one BR stands for Buy Rank."

$$TAI = BR \left(1 + \frac{FDA}{2(FDA) - CP} \right)$$

"Thanks Greg," said Rob. "I've tried it out and so far it works great. Remember when looking at the buy rank by itself, I said anytime it was positive it was good and above five it was great. The take action indicator is a little different. We want to take action (Time to Act) when it is between 10 and −5, be cautious (Wait) when it is between −5 and −10, and look at other opportunities (Bad Idea) if it is less than −10. If the TAI has a value above 10 it may still be okay to proceed with this prospect but a second review of the fifty-two week price chart with the fifty-day moving average is in order to see if the stock is still in a downward trend. We may be too early so we want to verify it (Get Ready) before we act."

"Here's what you are looking for on the TAI."

Rob wrote in his note pad and the following appeared on the screen.

"To get a better understanding of the Take Action Indicator I incorporated it into the VISIONS software. With VISIONS this information is readily available on the stock data page and on the VISIONS chart. You can sort and filter your prospect stock data by TAI. On the chart you can see how long the stock has been at each TAI value and be ready to take action once your prospect has traded in the VISIONS View V for a good number of days (20 is preferred). This makes it easy to decide which stock and option to add to your portfolio and which stocks in your portfolio you may want to sell."

"Here is a VISIONS chart that shows how SNDK was in a Time to Act state for 15 days and in the V for 29 days on December 6, 2004. It had a Gold $ score of 100 which is considered Ideal. A three or four

89

month **ATM** covered call would have been successful if executed at that time."

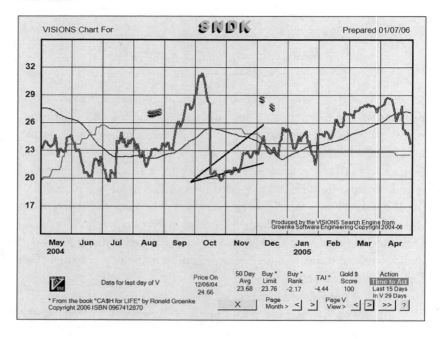

"The **VISIONS** View V is a window into how a stock is trading in relation to my Buy Limit and the 50 day moving average. It is truly unique and provides the information one needs to make better investment decisions. Here is how the **VISIONS** View V is constructed."

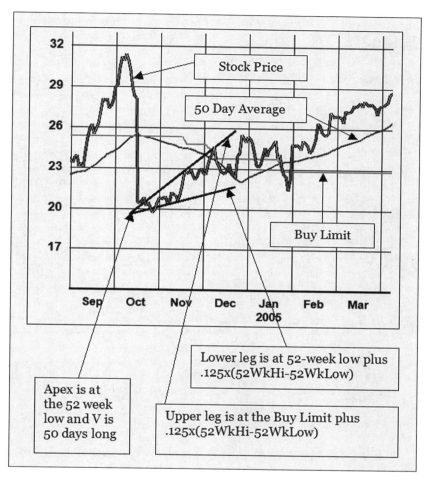

"The VISIONS Gold $ attempts to show where the best trading opportunities are. It is shown when the Gold $ Score is greater than or equal to the value selected. A score of 100 is considered Ideal.

"The Score is calculated as follows:

"10 * (# of up days) + 2 * (# of days in VISIONS View V) + (30 or 0, 30 if the stock is in the VISIONS View V or price is in 50 day average range, 0 if it is not).

The Ideal case is when a stock is trading in the VISIONS V View for 20 days, going up the last 3 days, and within 5% of the 50 day moving average. This is however not fool proof. Make sure the fundamentals of the company meet your selection criteria before you act.

Here is a graph of MFE which indicated an ideal situation on March 7, 2006.

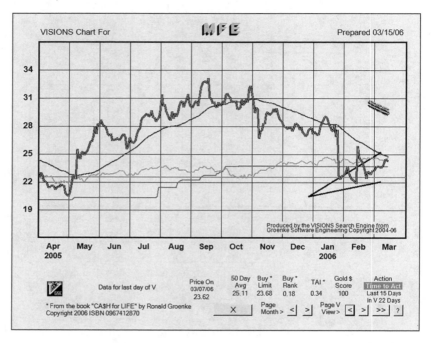

"Here is the chart for **SYMC**. This is one of the examples that was shown to the investment club. When the club made their investment in **SYMC** the **VISIONS** View V indicated a Bad Idea for over 150 days.

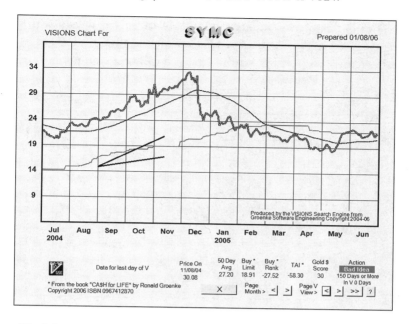

"In May 2005 the VISIONS View V indicated a Time to Act for 6 days. This is when I took action and executed a successful covered call."

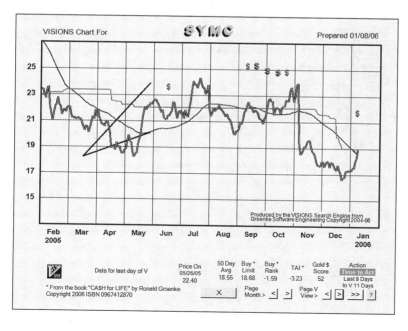

"The indicator was indicating Get Ready for 40 days at the end of 2005. The Gold $ had a value of 90, which is almost Ideal. Time to consider this prospect for another covered call or naked put."

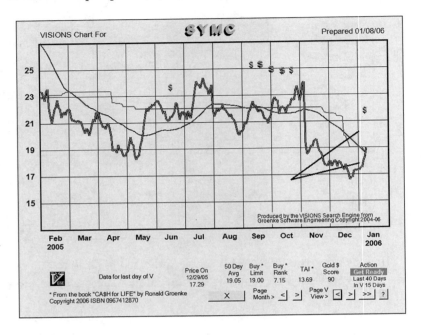

With excitement Jake jumped up and exclaimed, "Radio Shack! What does the Visions V predict about Radio Shack?'

"Sure," Rob responded. "I will key-in **RSH** for its current chart."

After a few seconds the following chart appeared.

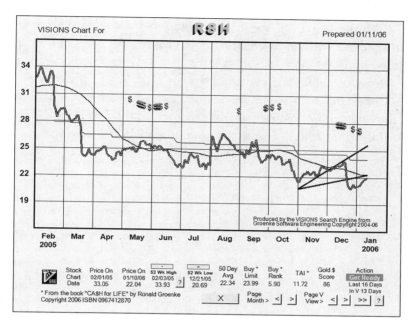

"Here it is Jake. Tell us what you see."

After quietly studying the cart for a few minutes Jake took a deep breath, exhaled slowly. "Well the Action indicator in the bottom right says "Get Ready." So it is premature to make an investment now."

"That's right," agreed Rob. "I would wait before making an investment in Radio Shack at this point. Perhaps consider a put. But keep in mind the Action indicator only applies to new investments. Since you already own the stock it would be OK to go ahead with selling a covered call provided the fundamentals are good on this particular stock. What else do you see?"

Jake was beginning to get more excited. "Why, I understand it now. This takes all the hassle out of trying to figure out what to do and when to do it. With the Visions V I'm guided to the right stocks at the right time. And then with calls and puts search engine I can find the best calls and puts for each stock that meets the Visions V criteria. Wow!

"Did you say you've incorporated this into your software?"

"Yes, it's all included in my software which I am now offering to investors for a 21-day free trial from my website. [**RonGroenke.com**] My goal is to help investors be successful. Like you said Jake, with the TAI, the VISIONS View V, and the Gold $, you have a number and a picture of when to act. This could give you the added advantage needed to improve the success rate for all your investments."

Rob closed his note pad Illustrator and the screen became a live scene of a cabin on a lake in Minnesota. Ice cycles hung from the eves of the cabin and a cold rain was blowing across the frozen lake. Looking at Greg he said, "Does it make you homesick, brother?"

14

Simulation with Taxes and Losses

One definition of an economist is somebody who sees something happen in practice and wonders if it will work in theory.
Ronald Reagan

The setting sun on the clear waters of the Caribbean was matched by the rising of a glorious full moon. Jake and Katie enjoyed the view as they walked across the top deck of the cruise ship where they were to meet Rob and Jean. Over the past year they had repeatedly sold calls on the 2000 shares of Radio Shack stock, their first venture in the options market. With the Professor's assistance they had developed a portfolio of over thirty stocks which met their investment criteria and had a good yield in call premiums. Part of the monthly premium income was used for living expenses and the remainder was reinvested.

"Hurry, come look at the dolphins," Jean called to from the port side of the deck. The dolphins seemed to be enjoying racing along with the fairly small luxury cruise ship. There were only 400 passengers and an equal number of staff and crew. The whole purpose of the cruise was the investment seminars sponsored by one of the major investment publications. Jake had written an article for the national magazine titled "The Professor's Money Tree" which resulted in Rob being invited to be one of the lecturers on the cruise.

"These are really posh accommodations," exclaimed Katie. "Now if I could just get these nautical terms right. Like how do you know which side is port and which side is starboard?"

The two couples enjoyed the beauty of the sky and the frolicking of the dolphins. Their destination was Grand Cayman. But the real purpose of the trip was to provide a pleasant setting for the financial seminars.

"I heard a bit of trivia once that helps me with those terms, port and starboard," said Rob. "And it has to do with the word 'posh' that you just used Katie. When cruise ships first started going out of London down the coast of Europe and through the straits of Gibraltar, the first class passengers wanted to be on the side of the ship with a view of the coast. Naturally they would be on the port or left side going down. Then on the return cruise home they would change to the staterooms on the right or starboard side of the ship so they would still have a view of the coast. The term 'port out starboard home' or simply posh, became synonymous with first class accommodations."

One of the staff came by with a tray of drinks and hors d'oeuvres. As they walked along the deck Jake commented to Rob, "You really got a lot of response last night on your lecture 'Make Your Own Dividends'. I could tell that was a real eye opener for most of the audience. What will you talk about in tonight's lecture?"

"You remember there was an important question asked the first night in the opening session that is typically not covered in these seminars. In fact the guy made the point that he had read a lot of books about making money in the stock market. All the systems he had read about never took into account that the market goes down as well as up, that you can and do have real losses in the stock market. I have developed a software program that simulates stock investments and the subsequent sell of covered calls. You can alter the various factors, including a stock loss, and see the resulting portfolio gain or loss over a period of time. My Illustrator works with the ships video system so I can run the simulation based on questions from the audience in real time."

"What about the Cedric Chart? Are you going to show that?" Jake had been amazed at the apparent accuracy of the Buy/Sell time line chart of unknown origin, perhaps made as early as the Civil War.

"Hmmm. The fat years, the lean years. It might be interesting to get the reaction of this sophisticated group of investors."

Their conversation was interrupted by the familiar ship's bell that indicated the captain was about to make an announcement.

"This is the Captain speaking. Tonight's lecture by Dr. Robert Gra-

CHAPTER 14 | SIMULATION WITH TAXES AND LOSSES

ham has been moved to the Main Theater to facilitate the increased demand. Dr. Charles Jackson's lecture on "Selecting the Right Mutual Fund" will now be held in Stateroom B."

* * *

Three seats had been reserved on the front row for Jake, Katie and Jean. Rob walked immediately onto the stage and was introduced by the MC, Kudlow Cramer.

"Ladies and Gentlemen. Professor Graham will speak tonight on the subject *Simulate Your Trading Plan.* As you know, last night's topic, *Creating* CA$H *for* LIFE, has been the main topic of conversation all day. I'm sure that accounts for the overflow crowd tonight."

A murmur went through the audience. "Yes, yes," the moderator continued. "I know some of you found last night's topic to be a little controversial, especially those of you associated with old line full service brokerage houses." As most of the audience laughed, recalling the professor's blunt talk about the individual investor's ability to manage his own investment account, Kudlow winked at Rob. Rob smiled in return but otherwise maintained a professional decorum.

"Please welcome once again Professor Robert Graham."

The standing ovation surprised Rob. He quickly motioned for the audience to be seated so he could begin his presentation.

"Before I initiate a trade I simulate its effect on my portfolio for the next three years out. If I am selling a call on a stock I own, I want to know the effect of tying up the underlying value of the long stock position. If I write a six-month call option I know that the stock is committed and the plan is that it will be called. If it is called the cash received for the underlying stock value is used to buy a new position from my prospect list and again write covered calls. If the stock is not called I need to make a basic decision. I will either liquidate my position in the stock because of changes in the company and the marketplace or I sell a new call option. Selling a new call option requires a decision as to the new strike price and months to expiration. On some of my stocks I have sold covered calls over a dozen times. As one three month or six month call option expires I sell a new one. That generates a powerful compounding effect.

"All of these factors can be easily simulated in a program I have developed for just this purpose.

"Last night I talked to you about creating dividends on stocks that don't pay dividends. That's the money tree effect: generating income by selling covered calls. It's nice to have an orchard of money trees. Each month you can pluck some fruit from some of the trees in your orchard.

"But . . ." Rob paused to be sure he had everyone's full attention. "But suppose some of the trees go bad. By that I mean suppose some of the stocks you select in your portfolio go down in value. What effect will that have on our plan to generate a high rate of return on our investment? That's the purpose of the simulation. We want to gain confidence that we can generate a high return even if some of our stocks go bad.

"It is important to set down a goal. In most cases option values follow the normal ups and downs of the market, so let's be realistic in our expected gains. Is 20% possible? Yes. Is 30% possible? Yes. Is 50% possible? Yes, a 50% gain in one year on your investments with options is possible because I've been there, done that! Okay, what is realistic? Let's pick a goal of 25%. Would you agree that a 25% return on your stock portfolio would be pretty good?

"Here is the plan. We'll keep it simple for illustration purposes. We are going to take $25000 and buy three different stocks and sell covered calls. I like to have income coming in each month so for the first month I will sell a one month call on one stock, a two month call on the second stock and a three month call on the third stock. We'll assume we are starting in January. In February and subsequent months we will sell three month calls.

"We start the simulation with an initial investment of $25000."

Rob punched the number into his Illustrator and it flashed on the three large screens, one directly in front of the audience and two on each side. "We need to make a couple of assumptions. First how much premium as a percentage of the stock price could you expect to get for a three month option? My experience has been that you can fairly easily get 10% return for three months. You will need to test this yourself by checking the call premiums on some of your favorite stocks. You should easily get this information from your online broker. Or go to **www.yahoo.com**. You may find it easier to get, say, 4% for one month than 10% for three months. It all depends on stock volatility. The higher the volatility the greater the premium. Anyway for our simulation we will use 3.3% a month or 10% for three months.

"Now the next assumption is stock loss. Unless you are absolutely brilliant and extremely lucky, you will pick some stocks that insist on going down in value rather than up. I will use a 15% loss factor. The simulator will sell two of my stocks each year for a combined loss of 15% of the beginning of year portfolio value. Does that seem reasonable?"

There were murmurs of agreement through out the room.

"Now there is one other factor we need to consider. What about taxes? At the end of each year I will have the simulation deduct 25% of the net income—call premiums less stock losses—from the portfolio to keep the tax man happy. For simplicity I have ignored commission expense and gains from stock appreciation. Commissions are low if you use a good online broker and would be more than off set by gains from stock appreciation. Also in this particular simulation we are not using the leverage available in margin accounts."

SIMULATION SETUP SUMMARY
PORTFOLIO GROWTH
THROUGH THE SELLING OF
COVERED CALLS FACTORS:

1. INITIAL INVESTMENT: $25,000

2. 10% PREMIUM PER QUARTER
   (3.3% PER MONTH)

3. ASSUMED STOCK LOSSES EACH YEAR OF 15%
   OF BEGINNING BALANCE

4. ASSUMED TAX OF 25% OF NET INCOME
   (PREMIUMS LESS LOSSES)

As Rob finished punching numbers in the Illustrator the following was shown on the screen:

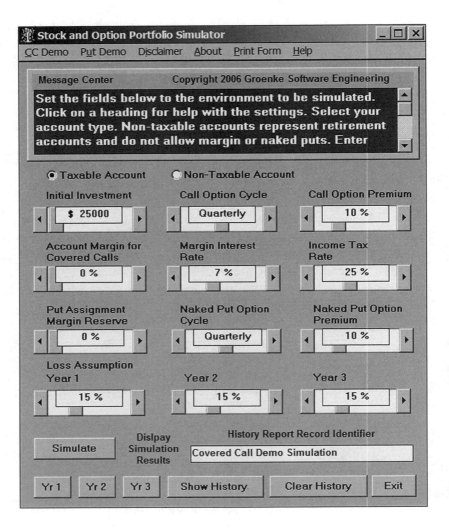

"OK. Are you ready? Here comes the simulation for the first six months."

YEAR ONE

MONTH	TRANSACTION	AMT	BAL	INC
JAN	INITIAL INVESTMENT	25000	25000	
	BUY A & SELL MAR CALLS	−12500	12500	
	OPTIONS SOLD AT 6.7 %	837	13337	
	BUY B & SELL APR CALLS	−10670	2667	
	OPTIONS SOLD AT 10 %	1067	3734	
	BUY C & SELL FEB CALLS	− 3734	-0-	
	OPTIONS SOLD AT 3.3 %	123	123	
	OPTION PREM INCOME JAN			2027
FEB	STK C CALLED OR EXPIRED	3734	3857	
	STK C SELL MAY CALLS	− 3857	-0-	
	OPTIONS SOLD AT 10 %	385	385	
	OPTION PREM INCOME FEB			385
MAR	STK A CALLED OR EXPIRED	12500	12885	
	STK A SELL JUN CALLS	12885	-0-	
	OPTIONS SOLD AT 10 %	1288	1288	
	OPTION PREM INCOME MAR			1288
APR	STK B CALLED OR EXPIRED	10670	11958	
	STK B SELL JUL CALLS	11958	-0-	
	OPTIONS SOLD AT 10 %	1195	1195	
	OPTION PREM INCOME APR			1195
MAY	STK C CALLED OR EXPIRED STK C	3857	5053	
	SELL AUG CALLS	−5053	-0-	
	OPTIONS SOLD AT 10 %	505	505	
	OPTION PREM INCOME MAY			505
JUNE	STK A CALLED OR EXPIRED	12885	13391	
	STK A SELL SEP CALLS	-13391	-0-	
	OPTIONS SOLD AT 10 %	1339	1339	
	OPTION PREM INCOME JUN			1339

"Let's go over this first six months and I think you will quickly get the hang of it. In January we make an initial investment in our brokerage account of $25,000. We buy three stocks, A, B & C, carefully selected from our prospect list. You recall last night I talked briefly about my system of ranking stocks and use of the TAI formula. Stock selection is very important but for tonight's discussion we are focusing on the three year simulation.

"For our first purchase of stock A we sell March calls for a premium of 6.7%. For simplicity we are assuming the strike price is the same as the purchase price when in reality the strike price would frequently be about 5 to 10% above the purchase price.

"The premium received of $837 is added to our account balance and used in the purchase of stocks B & C. Thus the compounding effect begins the very first month. On stock B we sell April calls and on stock C we sell February calls. In subsequent months all calls will be for three months. By staggering the calls the first month and then selling three month options we are able to have premium income each month.

"Each stock will either be called, in which case we receive cash, or the option will expire. Either event leaves us in position to repeat the process, selling additional calls and reinvesting at least part of the premium received.

"Now let's take a look at the last six months and portfolio value at year end."

MONTH	TRANSACTION	AMT	BAL	INC
JULY	STK B CALLED OR EXPIRED	11958	13297	
	STK B SELL OCT CALLS	-13297	-0-	
	OPTIONS SOLD AT 10 %	1329	1329	
	OPTION PREM INCOME JUL			1329
AUG	STK C CALLED OR EXPIRED	5053	6383	
	STK C SELL NOV CALLS	-6383	-0-	
	OPTIONS SOLD AT 10 %	638	638	
	OPTION PREM INCOME AUG			638
SEP	STK A SOLD AT LOSS (13391 − 1500)	11891	12529	
	NEW A SELL DEC CALLS	-10023	2505	
	OPTIONS SOLD AT 10 %	1002	3508	
	BUY D SELL DEC CALLS	-3508	-0-	
	OPTIONS SOLD AT 10 %	350	350	
	OPTION PREM INCOME SEP			1353
OCT	STK B SOLD AT LOSS (13297 − 2250)	11047	11398	
	NEW B SELL JAN CALLS	-11398	-0-	
	OPTIONS SOLD AT 10 %	1139	1139	
	OPTION PREM INCOME OCT			1139

NOV	STK C CALLED OR EXPIRED	6383	7523	
	STK C SELL FEB CALLS	-7523	-0-	
	OPTIONS SOLD AT 10 %	752	752	
	OPTION PREM INCOME NOV			752
DEC	A&D CALLED OR EXPIRED	13531	14284	
	STK A&D SELL MAR CALLS	-14284	-0-	
	OPTIONS SOLD AT 10 %	1428	1428	
	TAX RESERVE	-2408	-980	
	OPTION PREM INCOME DEC			1428
TOTAL PREMIUM INCOME YEAR ONE				13378

PORTFOLIO VALUE AT YEAR END		
	AMT	BALANCE
STOCK A & D	14284	14284
STOCK B	11398	25682
STOCK C	7523	33205
CASH (DEC PREMIUMS)	1428	34633
25% TAX ON NET INCOME (PREMIUMS LESS LOSSES)	-2408	32225
ASSUMED STOCK LOSSES		3750
GAIN AFTER TAX & LOSS		7220
RETURN ON INVESTMENT		28.90%

"Notice the transactions in September and October. In those months we incur stock market losses of $1500 and $2250, 15% of the beginning of year portfolio balance. These losses reflect real life experiences. No matter how careful you are there will be stock market losses. For simulation purposes we have just assumed we will lose 15% each year. These losses could occur because the stock price went down and we decided to sell the stock. Perhaps the stock no longer meets our stock selection criteria such as profitable quarters or volume of trades. Another way we could have a loss is when the market price goes down and we decide to sell calls at a lower strike price than our original purchase price. If that happens and the stock is called we again have a stock loss. In that case the loss may well be offset by premium income, but it is still a loss. A stock market strategy is only worthwhile if it can overcome those losses and still show a significant gain.

"Notice in December we deduct $2,408 for tax reserve. This is 25% of net income, $13,378 premium income less the $3,750 stock losses. Taxes are even more certain than stock market losses. It's best to just accept the fact that you are going to make money and you will need to pay taxes. As the quantity of premium income increases you will probably need to make quarterly payments to the IRS. Plan ahead. Set aside a reserve for taxes so you aren't caught in a situation of having to liquidate some investments to pay taxes.

"Finally, how did we do for the year? Even after taxes and market losses our portfolio value has grown to $32,225, all from the sell of call options. We are ignoring the possibility of stock market appreciation.

"Our portfolio growth of $7,225 represents a return on investment of 28.9%. Let's move on to year two."

Rob flashed all of year two and the summary onto the screens

YEAR TWO

MONTH	TRANSACTION	AMT	BAL	INC
JAN	BALANCE FORWARD		-980	
	STK B CALLED OR EXPIRED	11398	10418	
	STK B SELL APR CALLS	-10418	-0-	
	OPTIONS SOLD AT 10 %	1041	1041	
	OPTION PREM INCOME JAN			1041
FEB	STK C CALLED OR EXPIRED	7523	8565	
	STK C SELL MAY CALLS	- 8565	-0-	
	OPTIONS SOLD AT 10 %	856	856	
	OPTION PREM INCOME FEB			856
MAR	A&D CALLED OR EXPIRED	14284	15140	
	STK A SELL JUN CALLS	7570	7570	
	OPTIONS SOLD AT 10 %	757	8327	
	STK D SELL JUN CALLS	8327	-0-	
	OPTIONS SOLD AT 10 %	833	833	
	OPTION PREM INCOME MAR			1590
APR	STK B SOLD AT A LOSS (10418 – 1450)	8968	9801	
	STK B SELL JUL CALLS	-9801	-0-	
	OPTIONS SOLD AT 10 %	980	980	
	OPTION PREM INCOME APR			980

MAY	STK C CALLED OR EXPIRED STK C	8565	9545	
	SELL AUG CALLS	-9545	-0-	
	OPTIONS SOLD AT 10 %	954	954	
	OPTION PREM INCOME MAY			954
JUNE	A & D CALLED OR EXPIRED	15897	16852	
	STK A SELL SEP CALLS	-8426	8426	
	OPTIONS SOLD AT 10 %	843	9269	
	STK D SELL SEP CALLS	-9269	-0-	
	OPTIONS SOLD AT 10 %	927	927	1770
	OPTION PREM INCOME JUNE			
JULY	STK B CALLED OR EXPIRED	9801	10728	
	STK B SELL OCT CALLS	-10728	-0-	
	OPTIONS SOLD AT 10 %	1072	1072	
	OPTION PREM INCOME JUL			1072
AUG	STK C CALLED OR EXPIRED	9545	10617	
	STK C SELL NOV CALLS	-10617	-0-	
	OPTIONS SOLD AT 10 %	1062	1062	
	OPTION PREM INCOME AUG			1062
SEP	A&D CALLED OR EXPIRED	17695	18757	
	NEW A SELL DEC CALLS	9378	9378	
	OPTIONS SOLD AT 10 %	938	10316	
	NEW D SELL DEC CALLS	10316	-0-	
	OPTIONS SOLD AT 10 %	1031	1031	
	OPTION PREM INCOME SEP			1969
OCT	STK B CALLED OR EXPIRED	10728	11759	
	STK B SELL JAN CALLS	11759	-0-	
	OPTIONS SOLD AT 10 %	1176	1176	
	OPTION PREM INCOME OCT			1176
NOV	STK C SOLD AT A LOSS			
	(10617 - 3384)	7234	8410	
	STK C SELL FEB CALLS	-8410	-0-	
	OPTIONS SOLD AT 10 %	841	841	
	OPTION PREM INCOME NOV			841
DEC	A&D CALLED OR EXPIRED	19694	20535	
	NEW A SELL MAR CALLS	10268	10267	
	OPTIONS SOLD AT 10 %	1027	11294	
	NEW D SELL MAR CALLS	11294	-0-	
	OPTIONS SOLD AT 10 %	1129	1129	
	TAX RESERVE	2659	-1530	
	OPTION PREM INCOME DEC			2156
	TOTAL PREMIUM INCOME YEAR TWO			**15467**

PORTFOLIO VALUE AT YEAR END		
	AMT	BALANCE
STOCK A	10268	10268
STOCK B	11759	22027
STOCK C	8410	30437
STOCK D	11295	41732
CASH	1129	42861
25% TAX ON NET INCOME (PREMIUMS LESS LOSSES)	-2659	40202
ASSUMED STOCK LOSSES		4834
GAIN AFTER TAX & LOSS		7974
RETURN ON INVESTMENT		24.75%

"The key point here," Rob began, "is that the advantages of compounding are powerful but begin slowly. Our portfolio has grown by almost $8,000 or 24.75%. Accordingly we have larger stock losses and reserve for taxes ... Let's go on to year three."

YEAR THREE

MONTH	TRANSACTION	AMT	BAL	INC
JAN	BALANCE FORWARD B CALLED OR EXPIRED STK B SELL APR CALLS OPTIONS SOLD AT 10 % OPTION PREM INCOME APR	 11759 -10229 1023	-1530 10229 -0- 1023	 1023
FEB	STK C CALLED OR EXPIRED STK C SELL MAY CALLS OPTIONS SOLD AT 10 % OPTION PREM INCOME FEB	8410 - 9433 943	9433 -0- 943	 943
MAR	A&D CALLED OR EXPIRED STK A SELL JUN CALLS OPTIONS SOLD AT 10 % STK D SELL JUN CALLS OPTIONS SOLD AT 10 % NEW E SELL JUN CALLS OPTIONS SOLD AT 10 % OPTION PREM INCOME MAR	21562 11253 1125 -9902 990 -3465 346	22505 11252 12377 2475 3465 -0- 346	 2462
APR	STK B CALLED OR EXPIRED STK B SELL JUL CALLS OPTIONS SOLD AT 10 % OPTION PREM INCOME APR	10230 -10576 1057	10576 -0- 1057	 1057
MAY	STK C CALLED OR EXPIRED STK C SELL AUG CALLS OPTIONS SOLD AT 10 % OPTION PREM INCOME MAY	9433 -10490 1049	10490 -0- 1049	 1049

JUNE	A&D CALLED OR EXPIRED	24621	25670	
	STK A SELL SEP CALLS	-12835	12835	
	OPTIONS SOLD AT 10 %	1283	14118	
	STK D SELL SEP CALLS	-11295	2824	
	OPTIONS SOLD AT 10 %	1129	3953	
	STK E SELL SEP CALLS	-3953	-0-	
	OPTIONS SOLD AT 10 %	395	395	
	OPTION PREM INCOME JUN			2808
JULY	STK B SOLD AT LOSS (10756 – 3015)	7561	7956	
	NEW B SELL OCT CALLS	-7956	-0-	
	OPTIONS SOLD AT 10 % OPTION PREM INCOME JUL	795	795	795
AUG	STK C CALLED OR EXPIRED	10491	11286	
	STK C SELL NOV CALLS	-11286	-0-	
	OPTIONS SOLD AT 10 %	1128	1128	
	OPTION PREM INCOME AUG			1128
SEP	STK D SOLD AT LOSS (11295 – 3015)	8280	9408	
	NEW D SELL DEC CALLS	-6706	2702	
	OPTIONS SOLD AT 10 %	670	3372	
	A&E CALLED OR EXPIRED	16788	20160	
	STK A SELL DEC CALLS	-10478	9682	
	OPTIONS SOLD AT 10 %	1048	10730	
	STK E SELL DEC CALLS	-8584	2146	
	OPTIONS SOLD AT 10 %	858	3004	
	NEW F SELL DEC CALLS	-3004	-0-	
	OPTIONS SOLD AT 10 %	300	300	
	OPTION PREM INCOME SEP			2876
OCT	STK B CALLEDOR EXPIRED	7957	8257	
	STK B SELL JAN CALLS	-8257	-0-	
	OPTIONS SOLD AT 10 %	826	826	
	OPTION PREM INCOME OCT			826
NOV	STK C CALLEDOR EXPIRED	11286	12112	
	STK C SELL FEB CALLS	-12112	-0-	
	OPTIONS SOLD AT 10 %	1211	1211	
	OPTION PREM INCOME NOV			1211
DEC	A,D,E&F CALLED	28773	29984	
	NEW A SELL MAR CALLS	-11994	17990	
	OPTIONS SOLD AT 10 %	1199	19190	
	NEW D SELL MAR CALLS	-7676	11514	
	OPTIONS SOLD AT 10 %	768	12282	
	STK E SELL MAR CALLS	-9825	2456	
	OPTIONS SOLD AT 10 %	982	3438	
	STK F SELL MAR CALLS	-3438	-0-	
	OPTIONS SOLD AT 10 %	343	343	
	TAX RESERVE	3361	–3018	
	OPTION PREM INCOME DEC			3292
	TOTAL PREMIUM INCOME YEAR THREE			19470

PORTFOLIO VALUE AT YEAR END		
	AMT	BALANCE
STOCK A	11994	11994
STOCK B	8257	20251
STOCK C	12112	32363
STOCK D	7676	40039
STOCK E	9825	49864
STOCK F	3438	53302
CASH	343	53645
25% TAX ON NET INCOME (PREMIUMS LESS LOSSES)	-3361	50284
ASSUMED STOCK LOSSES		6030
GAIN AFTER TAX & LOSS		10079
RETURN ON INVESTMENT		25.07%

"Here we are at the end of year three. As the portfolio has grown we have diversified. We began with only three stocks and now have six. Of course, in real life, further diversification is possible and desirable.

"In three years we have doubled our portfolio from $25,000 to $50,000. The compounding effect is just beginning to take effect. In another three years the portfolio can grow to $100,000. After 10 years we could grow the $25,000 to $250,000 based on our assumptions of 10% premium for three months, 25% tax and 15% stock market losses."

Kudlow Cramer, the host and moderator, walked back on stage and shook hands with Rob as the audience burst into an appreciative round of applause.

"Professor, I have a few questions from the audience if you don't mind."

Rob nodded agreement.

"Question one: For self directed IRA's and other retirement plans on which taxes are deferred, what would be the simulated result without taxes?"

Rob quickly punched some numbers on his Illustrator and the following table flashed on the screen.

"I have run the simulation with different factors. If you avoid tax, as with a retirement account, and all other factors are the same as the simulation we just demonstrated, then the $25,000 grows to $61,540 in three years. Here are some interesting scenarios, beginning with the one demonstrated in detail tonight.

"The premium percentage is the call option premium divided by its underlying stock cost for the cycle indicated. For the last three simulations using funds borrowed from the brokerage account an interest rate of 7% is factored in as an expense."

COVERED CALL SIMULATION RESULTS						
Initial Invest.	Prem.	Cycle	Margin	Loss	Tax	3 YR Result
$25,000	10%	Quarterly	-0-	15%	25%	$50,284
$25,000	10%	Quarterly	-0-	15%	-0-	$61,540
$25,000	3%	Monthly	-0-	15%	-0-	$49,507
$25,000	4%	Monthly	40%	15%	25%	$73,406
$25,000	8%	Quarterly	40%	15%	25%	$48,965
$25,000	10%	Quarterly	40%	15%	25%	$62,861

"Next question: what about puts? The simulation only used covered calls."

"In my personal portfolio I use a strategy that combines both calls and puts to optimize return. For the beginning options investor I strongly recommend sticking with covered calls until you have gained experience.

"The simulation model allows you to include a certain level of put activity along with your covered calls. If we allow for example 40% of our margin to be used to cover the addition of naked puts to the previous simulation, the account balance after three years is $71,617 instead of the $50,284 shown. This additional gain is from selling puts and using the premium to invest in more covered calls.

"There are many combinations of calls and puts that one can consider. That is why the Stock and Option Portfolio Simulation software module is one of the most valuable tools to own since it makes all those what ifs understandable."

"Professor Graham, this has been a very illuminating presentation.

We have one final question. Are you a bull or a bear with respect to the next few years?"

Rob smiled. This was a question he could always expect. "I recently came across a chart that this group might find interesting. It's called 'Historical Buy & Sell Time Line' and goes from 1850 to 2018. I've been referring to it as the Cedric Chart because I learned about it from a newspaper column by Cedric Adams, a famous Minnesota newspaper columnist and radio personality very popular in the 1950's. Let's see if I can pull it up and flash it on the screen.

"Ah, here we go. I will leave it to you to decide the predictive value of the chart. I have personally been impressed with how 'right on' the chart has been in prior years. If it is accurate we are in for a few fat years. But lookout for the dip after 2007." (See Cedric Chart, opposite.)

Kudlow Cramer again broke in. "We have run out of time for additional questions. Thanks Rob for the wonderful insights into taking investment matters into our own hands. Perhaps I can get you to visit me on my weekly TV show. If anyone else has a question for Rob and does not get it answered before the end of the cruise, he has agreed to accept questions at **robgrahamphd@aol.com**."

Later that evening Jake and Katie invited Rob and Jean to join them on the balcony of their stateroom. Katie brought out mugs of decaf as they enjoyed the view of the full moon glistening on the Caribbean and reflected on the events of the past year.

Finally Jake broached a subject that had been on his mind lately. "Professor, the buzz about the possibility of continuous returns was really interesting. I didn't think we would ever get out of the auditorium there were so many questions. I know it works because I've been doing it for the past year. It's understandable that people will be a little skeptical about this concept of CA$H for LIFE. But how do you convince the skeptics? Do you have examples of what you've done on an ongoing basis?"

Rob smiled, gazing at the full moon. "Jake, yes, you have anticipated what I wanted to show you next. Tomorrow I will show you some of my ScoreCards."

Jake noticed that Katie and Jean were engrossed in their own conversation. As he tasted the coffee he noticed a meteor cross the

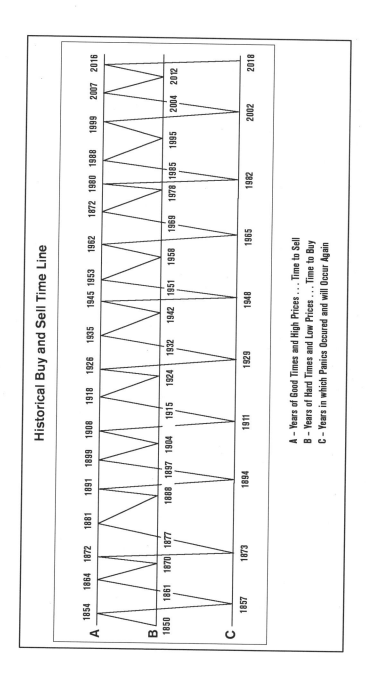

CEDRIC CHART

Historical Buy and Sell Time Line

A – Years of Good Times and High Prices . . . Time to Sell
B – Years of Hard Times and Low Prices . . . Time to Buy
C – Years in which Panics Occured and will Occur Again

sky. And in a moment of self reflection he realized he wasn't really aware of any of those events. His mind was focused on the professor's last comment. "I will show you some of my ScoreCards." What could this be?"

15

CA$H for LIFE

All our dreams can come true, if we have the courage to pursue them.
Walt Disney

The next day Jake and Rob met for a late breakfast in the main dinning room. "Jake, I usually do not show anyone what I am about to show you. The reason is that I do not like to boast. But since you were a little skeptical last night I thought this may give you the assurance that you need to believe in yourself. You really can do this."

"Here are what I called my ScoreCards last night. They are the detailed results of my trades in four different portfolios. I call these ScoreCards because that is what they represent. They show my performance with covered calls and naked puts as experienced in real life. These are some of the portfolios that generate my **CA$H for LIFE**.

"Why multiple ScoreCards? When I started on this journey generating cash on my investments I had one large portfolio. As it grew, some of the under performing stocks got lost in the numbers so to say. They were masked out by the good results of many others. Once I realized this I started new portfolios with the proceeds from stocks that were called. This way I was able to keep track of the results of various strategies and compare portfolio performance over time. This multiple portfolio concept has improved my success and I would suggest that you consider it as you start this journey."

"Here is the first ScoreCard which I started on January 7, 2005."

Rob handed Jake a printout of all the trades for ScoreCard #1 from January 10, 2005 to December 19, 2005.

Scorecard # 1

```
CA$H FOR LIFE INVESTMENT EXAMPLE HISTORY                         SCORECARD #1

THIS EXAMPLE IS FOR LEARNING PURPOSES ONLY. IT IS NOT A RECOMMENDATION.

INVESTMENT PLAN SUMMARY                                            12-19-05

DATE      TRANSACTION                              (+/- AMOUNT)     BALANCE
--------  -----------------------------------      ------------    ---------
01-07-05  INITIAL INVESTMENT                       +   50000.00    50000.00

01-10-05  BOUGHT 1000 SANDISK CORP      @ 24.130   -   24135.00    25865.00
          SOLD 10  SNDK FEB 22.50 CALLS @ 2.7500   +    2729.95    28594.95
          CALLED VALUE = 22480.25   SOLD % =  4.45 EXP % = 11.31

01-10-05  SOLD 10  SNDK FEB 20.00 PUTS @  .4000    +     379.98    28974.93

01-10-05  BOUGHT 900  AGILENT TECH     @ 22.530    -   20282.00     8692.93
          SOLD  9    A MAY 22.50 CALLS @ 2.1000    +    1869.97    10562.90
          CALLED VALUE = 20230.32   SOLD % =  8.96 EXP % =  9.22

01-10-05  BOUGHT 1000 MICRON TECH      @ 11.420    -   11425.00     -862.10
          SOLD 10    MU APR 11.00 CALLS @ 1.1000   +    1079.98      217.88
          CALLED VALUE = 10980.63   SOLD % =  5.56 EXP % =  9.45

02-18-05  1000 SNDK CALLED @ 22.50                 +   22480.25    22698.13

02-18-05  BOUGHT 1100 CREE INC         @ 23.200    -   25525.00    -2826.87
          SOLD 11  CREE JUN 22.50 CALLS @ 2.8000   +    3059.95      233.08
          CALLED VALUE = 24730.17   SOLD % =  8.87 EXP % = 11.98

02-18-05  SOLD 10  CREE JUN 17.50 PUTS @  .3500    +     329.98      563.06

04-12-05  SOLD 10    MU JUL 11.00 CALLS @  .3500   +     329.98      893.04

05-20-05  900 A CALLED @ 22.50                     +   20230.32    21123.36

05-20-05  SOLD 10    MU OCT  9.00  PUTS @  .3500   +     329.98    21453.34

05-24-05  BOUGHT 1000 SYMANTEC CORP    @ 22.110    -   22115.00     -661.66
          SOLD 10  SYMC OCT 22.50 CALLS @ 1.9000   +    1879.93     1218.27
          CALLED VALUE = 22480.25   SOLD % = 10.15 EXP % =  8.50

06-15-05  BOUGHT 1000 BOSTON SCIENTIFIC @ 28.700   -   28705.00   -27486.73
          SOLD 10    BSX NOV 27.50 CALLS @ 3.1000  +    3079.95   -24406.78
          CALLED VALUE = 27480.08   SOLD % =  6.46 EXP % = 10.73

06-15-05  SOLD 10    BSX AUG 25.00  PUTS @  .4000  +     379.98   -24026.80
```

Jake rubbed the shark scar on his arm again and exclaimed, "This looks a lot like the examples you have been sharing with me."

"Yes," Rob replied. "A lot of the examples have come from this very portfolio. I have not made any of this up. This is the real thing. Let me explain to you how it is organized.

"First, I apologize for the small print. I wanted to show you the exact format of the report as provided by the VISIONS software. So I took the trade report and copied it here for you. This way when you start using VISIONS you will be familiar with its content."

"I had $50,000 to invest, so with the help of the VISIONS Stock and Options Search Engine I was able to select three good companies to invest in."

"On January 10 I bought 1000 shares of SanDisk (SNDK) for $24.13 and sold 10 February $22.50 calls for $2.75. Notice how the balance in my account goes from $50,000 to $25,865.00 for the stock purchase and then to $28,594.95 after the call was sold."

"This was an ITM (In-The-Money) call because my assessment of the market at that time was down to flat. I also sold 10 SNDK February $20.00 naked puts for $.40 per share. I now had $28,974.93 in my account to work with."

"Then I bought 900 shares of Agilent Technology (A) for $22.53 and sold 9 May $22.50 calls for $2.10. This was an ATM (At-The-Money) call."

"The third trade consisted of buying 1000 shares of Micron Technology (MU) at $11.42 and selling 10 April $11.00 calls for $1.10 per share. This was also an ITM call. After these transactions were completed I had $217.88 left in my account."

"Any questions so far?"

"No," Jake replied. "It is very informative and easy to follow."

"Okay Jake, now lets move the calendar forward to the third Friday in February. This is the expiration day for the SNDK call options. SNDK was trading above the strike price so the 1000 shares in my account were called and $22480.25 was placed in my account on Monday, February 21. The SNDK February 20.00 put expired worthless."

"During this expiration week I was anticipating that SNDK would be called and I again used VISIONS to search for a new investment and it showed that Cree Inc (CREE) met my investment guidelines. Therefore on February 18 I bought 1100 shares of CREE at $23.20 and sold 11 CREE June $22.50 calls for $2.50. This was an ITM call since the market trend was still flat to down. I also sold 10 CREE June $17.50 puts for $.35 per share."

"After these trades were completed my account balance was $563.06. I now had calls expiring in April, May, and June."

"Any questions?"

"Yes," Jake replied. "Why did you sell another naked put?"

"Remember our previous discussion on my naked put strategy. I like to double Up. Since the SNDK put expired I now had some account margin available for more puts. After reviewing the VISIONS chart for CREE it showed a Take Action Indicator of Time To Act for 24 days on February 18, 2005. This is why I did the covered call and at the same time a naked put with a strike price almost $6.00 below the current market price and $8.00 lower then the Buy Limit. I felt this was a very safe trade.

"Now let's move forward to April, 2005"

"Micron Technology (MU) was trading below its April $11.00 strike price so the option expired. The person who bought this call in January now had nothing to show for their investment. They gambled and lost. We earned $1079.98 on this trade and now we can do it again."

"I sold 10 MU June $11.00 calls for $.35 per share. My account balance now was $893.04."

"As we move forward to May we can see that the Agilent (A) call was assigned at $22.50 placing $20,230.32 into my account."

"On May 20, 2005 I sold 10 MU October $9.00 puts for $.35 per share and on May 24 I bought 1000 shares of Symantec (SYMC) at $22.11 and sold 10 October $22.50 OTM (Out-Of-The-Money) calls. SYMC had just gone through a low in April and started moving up so I felt an OTM (Out-Of-The-Money) call was appropriate at this time to capture some upside if possible."

"Now two days prior to the June 17 option expiration date (third Friday of the month) I decided that since CREE was at $23.85 my stock would be called. I took action and bought 1000 shares of Boston Scientific (BSX) at $28.70 and sold ITM November $27.50 calls at $3.10. I also sold 10 BSX August $25.00 puts for $.40 netting $379.98."

"CREE was called on June 17 as expected and my account balance was at $703.37. At this point in 2005 I had a gain of 23.29% if all stock positions were called. Here is the summary."

Scorecard # 1 *(continued)*

```
STOCK VALUES AT STRIKE PRICE ON EXPIRATION DATE


07-15-05 1000 MU   CALLED @ 11.00        +        10980.63        10980.63
10-19-05 1000 SYMC CALLED @ 22.50        +        22480.25        33460.88
11-18-05 1000 BSX  CALLED @ 27.50        +        27480.08        60940.96


INITIAL INVESTMENT            50000.00
STOCK VALUE AT STRIKE PRICE   60940.96
CASH IN ACCOUNT                 703.37
TOTAL PORTFOLIO GAIN          11644.33
                                 23.29  %
```

"Now for the rest of the story."

"In the second half of 2005 you can see where I made an investment in Ebay Inc. (EBAY) after MU was called in July. I also had a significant cash balance ($25,364,78) in my account in November to cover a possible SigmaTel (SGTL) put assignment in December. SGTL went down in November when they changed their revenue guidance down due to supply and production issues."

"On December 16 I was assigned 1700 shares of SGTL at $15.00 per share as anticipated. Therefore on December 19 I sold 17 SGTL March $15.00 calls for $1.00 per share. This would earn me 6.67% in three months.

"On January 10, 2006 this ScoreCard (portfolio) was one year old and would have a gain of over 30% if all positions are called.

"The overall stock market during this period was flat and up a little. It was down significantly for the first nine months of 2005. In November it did get back to even. The Nasdaq (2175-2205) and S&P 500 (1212-1269) eked out a small gain for the year. The Dow 30 (10783-10718) was down 65 points for the year.

"During this same period the covered call and naked put Score-Card #1 gained over 30%.

"Was this just luck? I think not. This result was obtained through excellent stock and option analysis and selection. VISIONS was the main tool that was used to get the data that made the analysis possible in a timely fashion."

Scorecard # 1 (continued)

```
07-15-05  1000 MU    CALLED @ 11.00                    +      10980.63      11684.00

07-15-05  BOUGHT 300  EBAY              @ 35.100        -      10535.00       1149.00
          SOLD  3  EBAY OCT 35.00 CALLS @ 2.7000        +        794.98       1943.98
          CALLED VALUE = 10480.65   SOLD % =  7.03    EXP % =  7.54

08-22-05  SOLD 17  SGTL DEC 15.00  PUTS @ .7000         +       1169.96       3113.94

10-21-05  1000 SYMC CALLED @ 22.50                      +      22480.25      25594.19
10-21-05  300  EBAY CALLED @ 35.00                      +      10480.65      36074.84

10-24-05  BOUGHT 1000 MICRON TECHNOLOGY @ 12.460        -      12465.00      23609.84
          SOLD 10    MU JAN 12.50 CALLS @ .9500         +        934.98      24544.82
          CALLED VALUE = 12480.58   SOLD % =  7.62    EXP % =  7.50

10-24-05  SOLD  4  SGTL DEC 12.50  PUTS @ .5000         +        184.99      24729.81

11-21-05  SOLD 10   BSX JAN 27.50 CALLS @  .6500        +        634.97      25364.78

12-16-05  BUY 1700 SGTL 15.00                           -      25519.00       -154.22

12-19-05  SOLD 17  SGTL MAR 15.00 CALLS @ 1.0000        +       1682.19       1527.97
12-19-05  SOLD 10  CREE MAR 22.50 PUTS @  .5500         +        534.98       2062.95

STOCK VALUES AT STRIKE PRICE ON EXPIRATION DATE

01-20-06  1000 BSX   CALLED @ 27.50                     +      27480.08      27480.08
01-20-06  1000 MU    CALLED @ 12.50                     +      12480.50      39960.58
03-17-06  1700 SGTL  CALLED @ 15.00                     +      25480.15      65440.73


INITIAL INVESTMENT                 50000.00
STOCK VALUE AT STRIKE PRICE        65440.73
CASH IN ACCOUNT                     2062.95
TOTAL PORTFOLIO GAIN               17503.68
                                      35.01  %
```

"One may conclude that if you follow the company selection guidelines, the principles of when to act using the **VISIONS** View V take action indicator, and the process of taking and compounding a number of gains over time one may achieve the success demonstrated here and generate CA$H for LIFE.

"Here is a summary by company for your review. It is in the same format as the examples provided earlier. Again CE means Call Expired, PE means Put Expired, CA means Call Assigned, PA means Put Assigned, CO means Call Open (waiting for strike date), PO means Put Open (waiting for strike date), and P means Plan assignment."

Scorecard # 1 *(continued)*

```
HISTORY BY STOCK POSITION

SANDISK CORP               SNDK SWQ JAN APR JUL OCT
01-10-05 B    1000  24.13            24135.00  -24135.00
01-10-05 S 10 FEB  22.50   2.75      2729.95  -21405.05 CA
01-10-05 S 10 FEB  20.00    .40       379.98  -21025.07 PE
02-18-05 C    1000  22.50            22480.25   1455.18 <
                                     GAIN/LOSS     6.47 %

AGILENT                       A    A FEB MAY AUG NOV
01-10-05 B     900  22.53            20282.00  -20282.00
01-10-05 S  9 MAY  22.50   2.10      1869.97  -18412.03 CA
05-20-05 C     900  22.50            20230.32   1818.29 <
                                     GAIN/LOSS     8.98 %

MICRON TECHNOLOGY            MU   MU JAN APR JUL OCT
01-10-05 B    1000  11.42            11425.00  -11425.00
01-10-05 S 10 APR  11.00   1.10      1079.98  -10345.02 CE
04-12-05 S 10 JUL  11.00    .35       329.98  -10015.04 CA
05-20-05 S 10 OCT   9.00    .35       329.98   -9685.06 PE
07-15-05 C    1000  11.00            10980.63   1295.57 <
                                     GAIN/LOSS    11.79 %


10-24-05 B    1000  12.46            12465.00  -12465.00
10-24-05 S 10 JAN  12.50    .95       934.96  -11530.04 CO
01-20-06 P    1000  12.50            12480.50    950.46 <
                                     GAIN/LOSS     7.61 %

CREE INC                   CREE CQR MAR JUN SEP DEC
02-18-05 B    1100  23.20            25525.00  -25525.00
02-18-05 S 11 JUN  22.50   2.80      3059.95  -22465.05 CA
02-18-05 S 10 JUN  17.50    .35       329.98  -22135.07 PE
06-17-05 C    1100  22.50            24730.17   2595.10 <
                                     GAIN/LOSS    10.49 %
12-19-05 S 10 MAR  22.50    .55       534.98   3130.08 PO

SYMANTEC CORP              SYMC SYQ JAN APR JUL OCT
05-24-05 B    1000  22.11            22115.00  -22115.00
05-24-05 S 10 OCT  22.50   1.90      1879.93  -20235.07 CA
10-21-05 C    1000  22.50            22480.25   2245.18 <
                                     GAIN/LOSS    10.15 %

BOSTON SCIENTIFIC CORP     BSX BSX FEB MAY AUG NOV
06-15-05 B    1000  28.70            28705.00  -28705.00
06-15-05 S 10 NOV  27.50   3.10      3079.95  -25625.05 CE
06-15-05 S 10 AUG  25.00    .40       379.98  -25245.07 PE
11-21-05 S 10 JAN  27.50    .65       634.97  -24610.09 CO
01-21-06 P    1000  27.50            27480.08   2869.98 <
                                     GAIN/LOSS    10.44 %
```

(Continued next page)

Scorecard # 1 *(continued)*

```
EBAY INC                        EBAY XBA JAN APR JUL OCT
07-15-05 B     300   35.10           10535.00  -10535.00
07-15-05 S   3 OCT   35.00   2.70      794.98   -9740.02 CA
10-21-05 C     300   35.00           10480.65     740.63 <
                                     GAIN/LOSS      7.06 %

SIGMATEL                        SGTL UGO MAR JUN SEP DEC
08-22-05 S  17 DEC   15.00    .70     1169.96    1169.96 PA
10-24-05 S   4 DEC   12.50    .50      184.99    1354.95 PE
12-16-05 B    1700   15.00           25519.00  -24164.05
12-19-05 S  17 MAR   15.00   1.00     1682.22  -22481.83 CO
03-17-06 P    1700   15.00           25480.15    2998.32 <
                                     GAIN/LOSS     11.76 %
```

"Additional ScoreCards (#2, 3, 4) are provided here for your review. They are updated over time and the current status can be obtained by selecting the Now ScoreCards function on the **VISIONS** software opening page." You can get the software from my website, **RonGroenke.com**.

"ScoreCards 2 and 4 follow the same strategy as ScoreCard #1. Note the **ITM** or **ATM** strategy.

"ScoreCard #3 is somewhat different. It demonstrates what can be achieved by investing only in **ETF**'s (Exchange Traded Funds).

"The strategy here is to try and generate a return of 1% per month with some downside protection by selling mainly **ITM** (In-The-Money) calls on a variety of **ETF**'s.

"This is truly an income generating account since cash is withdrawn periodically.

"This is a unique example in that it demonstrates that the CA$H for LIFE concept is real and can implemented by most investors.

"So Jake, What do think?"

Jake had a big smile on his face as he responded, "I now believe that this is possible and can't wait to get home to work on my plan to generate CA$H for LIFE."

"Thanks professor for all your patience with me. I am truly grateful that you have shared all of this with us."

"No problem." Rob said. "I just like to see people happy."

* * *

Scorecard # 2

```
CA$H FOR LIFE INVESTMENT EXAMPLE HISTORY                    SCORECARD #2

THIS EXAMPLE IS FOR LEARNING PURPOSES ONLY. IT IS NOT A RECOMMENDATION.

INVESTMENT PLAN SUMMARY                                        11-21-05

DATE      TRANSACTION                              (+/- AMOUNT)    BALANCE
--------  ----------------------------------------  ------------  -----------
06-20-05  INITIAL INVESTMENT                       +   50000.00    50000.00

06-20-05  BOUGHT 1000 POLYCOM INC       @ 17.180   -   17185.00    32815.00
          SOLD 10  PLCM OCT 17.50 CALLS @ 1.2000   +    1179.98    33994.98
          CALLED VALUE = 17480.42   SOLD % =  8.58  EXP % =  6.86

06-20-05  SOLD 10  PLCM OCT 15.00  PUTS @ .4000    +     379.98    34374.96

06-20-05  BOUGHT 900  EGL INC          @ 20.220    -   18203.00    16171.96
          SOLD  9  EAGL NOV 20.00 CALLS @ 2.2000   +    1959.96    18131.92
          CALLED VALUE = 17980.40   SOLD % =  9.54  EXP % = 10.76

06-20-05  SOLD  6  EAGL NOV 17.50  PUTS @ .8500    +     494.98    18626.90

06-20-05  BOUGHT 500  INVESTORS FIN SVC @ 39.380   -   19695.00    -1068.10
          SOLD  5  IFIN OCT 40.00 CALLS @ 2.9000   +    1434.97      366.87
          CALLED VALUE = 19980.33   SOLD % =  8.73  EXP % =  7.28

10-21-05  BUY 1000 PLCM @ 15.00                    -   15019.00   -14652.13

10-24-05  SOLD 1000 PLCM @ 15.02                   +   15014.40      362.27
10-24-05  SOLD 10  PLCM JAN 17.50 CALLS @ .2500    +     234.99      597.26
10-24-05  SOLD  5  IFIN JAN 40.00 CALLS @ 1.2500   +     609.98     1207.24
10-24-05  SOLD  5  IFIN JAN 32.40  PUTS @ .6500    +     309.99     1517.23

11-18-05  900 EAGL CALLED @ 20.00                  +   17480.40    18997.63

11-21-05  BOUGHT 400  BIOGEN           @ 45.330    -   18137.00      860.63
          SOLD  4  BIIB APR 45.00 CALLS @ 5.0000   +    1984.96     2845.59
          CALLED VALUE = 17980.40   SOLD % = 10.08  EXP % = 10.94

11-21-05  SOLD  5  SYMC JAN 17.50  PUTS @ .5500    +     259.99     3105.58

STOCK VALUES AT STRIKE PRICE ON EXPIRATION DATE

01-20-06  1000 PLCM CALLED @ 17.50                 +   17480.42    17480.42
01-20-06  500  IFIN CALLED @ 40.00                 +   19980.33    37460.75
01-20-06  400  BIIB CALLED @ 45.00                 +   17980.40    55441.15


INITIAL INVESTMENT            50000.00
STOCK VALUE AT STRIKE PRICE   55441.15
CASH IN ACCOUNT                3105.58
TOTAL PORTFOLIO GAIN           8546.73
                                17.09  %
```

(Continued next page)

Scorecard # 2 *(continued)*

```
HISTORY BY STOCK POSITION

POLYCOM INC                      POLY QHD JAN APR JUL OCT
06-20-05 B    1000   17.18            17185.00  -17185.00
06-20-05 S 10 OCT    17.50   1.20      1179.98  -16005.02 CE
06-20-05 S 10 OCT    15.00    .40       379.98  -15625.04 PA
10-21-05 B    1000   15.00            15019.00  -30644.04
10-24-05 S    1000   15.02            15014.40  -15629.64 <
10-24-05 S 10 JAN    17.50    .25       234.99  -15394.65 CO
01-20-06 P    1000   17.50            17480.42    2085.77 <
                                     GAIN/LOSS     12.13 %

EGL INC                          EAGL KUF FEB MAY AUG NOV
06-20-05 B     900   20.22            18203.00  -18203.00
06-20-05 S  9 NOV    20.00   2.20      1959.96  -16243.04 CA
06-20-05 S  6 NOV    17.50    .85       494.98  -15748.06 PE
11-18-05 C     900   20.00            17980.40    2232.34 <
                                     GAIN/LOSS     12.41 %

INVESTORS FIN SERVICES           IFIN FLQ JAN APR JUL OCT
06-20-05 B     500   39.38            19695.00  -19695.00
06-20-05 S  5 OCT    40.00   2.90      1434.97  -18260.03 CE
10-24-05 S  5 JAN    40.00   1.25       609.98  -17650.05 CO
10-24-05 S  5 JAN    32.50    .65       309.99  -17340.06 PO
01-20-06 P     500   40.00            19980.33    2640.27 <
                                     GAIN/LOSS     13.40 %

BIOGEN IDEC INC                  BIIB IDK JAN APR JUL OCT
11-21-05 B     400   45.33            18137.00  -18137.00
11-21-05 S  4 APR    45.00   5.00      1984.92  -16152.08 CO
04-21-06 P     400   45.00            17980.40    1828.32 <
                                     GAIN/LOSS     10.16 %

SYMANTEC CORP                    SYMC SYQ JAN APR JUL OCT
11-21-05 S  5 JAN    17.50    .55       259.99     259.99 PO
```

Scorecard # 3

```
CA$H FOR LIFE INVESTMENT EXAMPLE HISTORY                    SCORECARD #3

THIS EXAMPLE IS FOR LEARNING PURPOSES ONLY. IT IS NOT A RECOMMENDATION.

STRATEGY - EARN 10% A YEAR USING ETF'S. SELL IN-THE-MONEY CALLS PROVIDING
           5-8% DOWNSIDE PROTECTION. SHORT TERM INCOME ACCOUNT. CASH IS
           WITHDRAWN SO GAINS DO NOT COMPOUND.

INVESTMENT PLAN SUMMARY                                     12-19-05

DATE      TRANSACTION                          (+/- AMOUNT)      BALANCE
-------   -----------------------------------  ------------   -----------
07-01-05  INITIAL INVESTMENT                   +   200000.00    200000.00

07-01-05  BOUGHT 900  SOFTWARE HLDR    @ 35.300 -    31775.00   168225.00
          SOLD  9   SWH NOV 35.00 CALLS @ 1.7500 +   1556.47    169781.47
          CALLED VALUE = 31479.95   SOLD % = 3.97 EXP % =  4.89

07-01-05  BOUGHT 2000 SEMICONDUCTOR HLDR@ 33.80 -    67605.00   102176.47
          SOLD 20   SMH NOV 32.50 CALLS @ 2.8500 +   5664.91    107841.38
          CALLED VALUE = 64978.83   SOLD % = 4.49 EXP % =  8.37

07-01-05  BOUGHT 3000 NASDAQ 100 TRUST @ 36.730 -   110195.00    -2353.62
          SOLD 30   QQQQ DEC 36.00 CALLS @ 2.4500 +   7299.87     4946.25
          CALLED VALUE =107977.39   SOLD % = 4.61 EXP % =  6.62

07-01-05  CASH WITHDRAWAL                      -     4900.00        46.25

11-18-05  900  SWH  CALLED @  35.00           +    31479.95    31526.20
11-18-05  2000 SMH  CALLED @  32.50           +    64978.83    96505.03

11-21-05  BOUGHT 300  OIL SERVICE HLDR @ 120.040 -  36017.00    60488.03
          SOLD  3   OIH JAN 115.0 CALLS @ 9.3000 +   2774.95    63262.98
          CALLED VALUE = 34479.85   SOLD % = 3.43 EXP % =  7.70

11-21-05  BOUGHT 1000 SOFTWARE HLDR    @ 37.350 -   37355.00    25907.98
          SOLD 10   SWH FEB 37.50 CALLS @ 1.1000 +   1084.98    26992.96
          CALLED VALUE = 37479.75   SOLD % = 3.23 EXP % =  2.90

11-21-05  BOUGHT 700  SEMICONDUCTORHLDR @ 36.480 -  25541.00     1451.96
          SOLD  7   SMH FEB 35.00 CALLS @ 2.5500 +   1769.97     3221.93
          CALLED VALUE = 24480.18   SOLD % = 2.77 EXP % =  6.93

11-21-05  CASH WITHDRAWAL                      -     3000.00       221.93

12-16-05  3000 QQQQ CALLED @  36.00           +   107977.39   108199.32
```

(Continued next page)

CA$H FOR LIFE

Scorecard # 3 *(continued)*

```
12-19-05  BOUGHT 700  NASDAQ 100 TRUST  @ 41.580      -   29111.00    79088.32
          SOLD  7  QQQQ MAR 41.00 CALLS @ 1.8000      +    1244.98    80333.30
          CALLED VALUE = 28680.04   SOLD % =  2.79  EXP % =  4.27

12-19-05  BOUGHT 400  RETAIL HOLDERS TR @ 98.600      -   39445.00    40888.30
          SOLD  4  RTH JAN 100.0 CALLS @ 1.3000       +     504.99    41393.29
          CALLED VALUE = 39979.66   SOLD % =  2.63  EXP % =  1.28

12-19-05  BOUGHT 200  BIOTECH HOLDERS TR@ 200.300     -   40065.00     1328.29
          SOLD  2  BBH APR 185.0 CALLS @22.1000       +    4404.93     5733.22
          CALLED VALUE = 36979.76   SOLD % =  3.29  EXP % = 10.99

12-19-05  CASH WITHDRAWAL                             -    5000.00      733.22

STOCK VALUES AT STRIKE PRICE ON EXPIRATION DATE

01-20-06  300  OIH  CALLED @ 115.00                  +   34479.85    34479.85
01-20-06  400  RTH  CALLED @ 100.00                  +   39979.66    74459.51
02-17-06 1000  SWH  CALLED @  37.50                  +   37479.75   111939.26
02-17-06  700  SMH  CALLED @  35.00                  +   24480.18   136419.44
03-17-06  700  QQQQ CALLED @  41.00                  +   28680.04   165099.48
04-21-06  200  BBH  CALLED @ 185.00                  +   36979.76   202079.24


INITIAL INVESTMENT              200000.00
STOCK VALUE AT STRIKE PRICE     202079.24
CASH IN ACCOUNT                    733.22
CASH WITHWRAWN (INCOME)          12900.00
TOTAL PORTFOLIO GAIN             15712.46
                                    7.86  %
```

126

Scorecard # 3 *(continued)*

```
HISTORY BY STOCK POSITION

SOFTWARE HOLDERS TRUST          SWH SWH       ALL MONTHS
07-01-05 B      900   35.30          31775.00  -31775.00
07-01-05 S  9 NOV   35.00   1.75      1556.47  -30218.53 CA
11-18-05 C      900   35.00          31479.95    1261.42 <
11-21-05 B     1000   37.35          37355.00  -36093.58
11-21-05 S 10 FEB   37.50   1.10      1084.96  -35008.62 CO
02-17-06 P     1000   37.50          37479.75    2471.13 <
                                GAIN/LOSS      6.59 %

SEMICONDUCTOR HLDRS TRUST       SMH SMH       ALL MONTHS
07-01-05 B     2000   33.80          67605.00  -67605.00
07-01-05 S 20 NOV   32.50   2.85      5664.91  -61940.09 CA
11-18-05 C     2000   32.50          64978.83    3038.74 <
                                GAIN/LOSS      4.67 %

11-21-05 B      700   36.48          25541.00  -25541.00
11-21-05 S  7 FEB   35.00   2.55      1769.93  -23771.07 CO
02-17-06 P      700   35.00          24480.18     709.11 <
                                GAIN/LOSS      2.89 %

OIL SERVICE HOLDERS TRUST       OIH OIH       ALL MONTHS
11-21-05 B      300  120.04          36017.00  -36017.00
11-21-05 S  3 JAN  115.00   9.30      2774.89  -33242.11 CO
01-20-06 P      300  115.00          34479.85    1237.74 <
                                GAIN/LOSS      4.12 %

NASDAQ 100 TRUST                QQQQ QQQ      ALL MONTHS
07-01-05 B     3000   36.73         110195.00 -110195.00
07-01-05 S 30 DEC   36.00   2.45      7299.88 -102895.12 CA
12-16-05 C     3000   36.00         107977.39    5082.27 <
                                GAIN/LOSS      4.70 %

12-19-05 B      700   41.58          29111.00  -29111.00
12-19-05 S  7 MAR   41.00   1.80      1244.98  -27866.02 CO
03-17-06 P      700   41.00          28680.04     814.02 <
                                GAIN/LOSS      2.83 %

ML RETAIL HOLDERS TRUST         RTH RTH       ALL MONTHS
12-19-05 B      400   98.60          39445.00  -39445.00
12-19-05 S  4 JAN  100.00   1.30       504.99  -38940.01 CO
01-20-06 P      400  100.00          39979.66    1039.65 <
                                GAIN/LOSS      2.63 %

ML BIOTECH HOLDERS TRUST        BBH BBH       ALL MONTHS
12-19-05 B      200  200.30          40065.00  -40065.00
12-19-05 S  2 APR  185.00  22.10      4404.93  -35660.07 CO
04-21-06 P      200  185.00          36979.76    1319.69 <
                                GAIN/LOSS      3.56 %
```

Scorecard # 4

```
CA$H FOR LIFE INVESTMENT EXAMPLE HISTORY                    SCORECARD #4

THIS EXAMPLE IS FOR LEARNING PURPOSES ONLY. IT IS NOT A RECOMMENDATION.

INVESTMENT PLAN SUMMARY                                      11-21-05

DATE      TRANSACTION                               (+/- AMOUNT)      BALANCE
--------  ------------------------------------      ------------      ----------
11-09-05  INITIAL INVESTMENT                        +    60000.00      60000.00

11-09-05  BOUGHT 1000 ALTERA CORP      @ 17.060     -    17065.00      42935.00
          SOLD 10  ALTR MAR 17.50 CALLS @ 1.2000    +     1184.95      44119.95
          CALLED VALUE = 17480.42   SOLD % =  9.37  EXP % =  6.94

11-09-05  BOUGHT 500  BIOMET INC       @ 36.370     -    18190.00      25929.95
          SOLD  5  BMET JAN 35.00 CALLS @ 3.2000    +     1584.94      27514.89
          CALLED VALUE = 17480.42   SOLD % =  4.81  EXP % =  8.71

11-09-05  SOLD  5  BMET JAN 32.50 PUTS @ .9500      +      459.98      27974.87

11-09-05  BOUGHT 1000 QLOGIC CORP      @ 30.780     -    30785.00      -2810.13
          SOLD 10  QLGC JAN 30.00 CALLS @ 2.5000    +     2484.90       -325.23
          CALLED VALUE = 29980.00   SOLD % =  5.45  EXP % =  8.07

11-09-05  SOLD  5  QLGC JAN 27.50 PUTS @ .7500      +      359.98         34.75

STOCK VAUES AT STRIKE PRICE ON EXPIRATION DATE

03-17-06  1000 ALTR CALLED @ 17.50                  +    17480.42      17480.42
01-20-06  500  BMET CALLED @ 35.00                  +    17480.42      34960.84
01-20-06  1000 QLGC CALLED @ 30.00                  +    29980.00      64940.84

INITIAL INVESTMENT             60000.00
STOCK VALUE AT STRIKE PRICE    64940.84
CASH IN ACCOUNT                   34.75
TOTAL PORTFOLIO GAIN            4975.59
                                  8.29  %
HISTORY BY STOCK POSITION

ALTERS CORP                  ALTR LTQ MAR JUN SEP DEC
11-09-05 B    1000  17.06        17065.00  -17065.00
11-09-05 S 10 MAR   17.50  1.20   1184.95  -15880.05 CO
03-17-06 P    1000  17.50        17480.42    1600.37 <
                             GAIN/LOSS        9.15 %

BIOMET INC                   BMET BIQ JAN APR JUL OCT
11-09-05 B     500  36.37        18190.00  -18190.00
11-09-05 S  5 JAN   35.00  3.20   1584.94  -16605.06 CO
11-09-05 S  5 JAN   32.50  .95     459.98  -16145.08 PO
01-20-06 P     500  35.00        17480.42    1335.34 <
                             GAIN/LOSS        7.63 %

QLOGIC CORP                  QLGC QLQ JAN APR JUL OCT
11-09-05 B    1000  30.78        30785.00  -30785.00
11-09-05 S 10 JAN   30.00  2.50   2484.90  -28300.10 CO
11-09-05 S  5 JAN   27.50 27.50    359.98  -27940.12 PO
01-20-06 P    1000  30.00        29980.00    2039.88 <
                             GAIN/LOSS        6.80 %
```

Now that you've read CA$H for LIFE You can meet professor Rob Graham in person at one of his seminars. Go to his website— **RonGroenke.com**—to find out about future seminars and download a 21-day free VISIONS trial. Below are comments from VISIONS software users and seminar attendees.

More Comments from Investors

I took leave from work, had to pay a premium for an airline ticket, and came all the way across the country for Ron's seminar (which took a full day). It was worth it all! Best investment I've ever made!!! One that's going to continue to pay off for the rest of my life! THANKS RON!

Robert Jamison
Sierra Vista, AZ

The seminar/workshop was well executed and very helpful in demonstrating the impressive scope and power of VISIONS. One could really appreciate the many thoughful features Ron has built in to make the process of finding good covered call opportunities much easier. Most of all, I felt the detailed examples and generous supporting information convincingly validated the effectiveness of his unique options strategies.

Richard Bradshaw
La Jolla, CA

The seminar was very informative and presented calls and puts in a simple and easy to follow format. *Cash for Life* is an essential book for any investor. Ron seems to plan for and share improvements as they evolve. Y'all were great hosts!

Wil Wilhite
Arkansas

After applying Ron Groenke's strategies, I feel Julius Caesar-like: I came, I saw, I conquered COVERED CALLS and NAKED PUTS.

Dr. Stan Cassel, D.V.M.
Nebraska

After coming to the seminar (which was fantastic) I have taken my knowledge from the book and multiplied it 100% because of all the fabulous explanations and "real life" scenarios. Ron reviewed his philosophies—why he did what he did—and also reviewed his mistakes. I really loved how he used the software and showed us where to get information, how to maneuver the software.

Beth Anderson
Florida

Excellent overall course. Appreciate amount of time put in to software. These ideas have worked for me for years. VISIONS software keeps it better organized and makes finding prospects easier. I highly recommend *Cash for Life.*

Robert Tyburski
Oklahoma

I've been trading covered calls for over two decades. Since reading Ron's book and using his system, I've been placing more trades and getting a better return. As an engineer, I always search for the easiest, most effective method in whatever I undertake and Ron's system is elegant in its simplicity. I highly recommend *Cash for Life* and VISIONS software.

Robert Bickford
Texas

Ron has solved many of the problems we face as investors but don't have the time or knowledge to solve for ourselves. I highly recommend *Cash for Life* and especially the seminar for all levels of investors!

Everett Cilla, DDS
Michigan

Ron, you certainly know your topic. With your math/programming background, and a calm, controlled teaching style, you make class most enjoyable as well as informative. This is one of the best classes for someone wanting to earn passive income. Keep up the good work Thank you.

Russ Morris
Seminole, FL

The best in the business. Great seminar. It should be named "Covered Calls Made Easy"!

Douglas Bruce
Laredo, TX

Ron teaches wealth accumulation through cash flow instead of speculation (not trying to predict the direction of the stock).

Ernest Gavalda
Miami, FL

I am extremely new to the world of options trading and your book and the seminar opened my eyes to a rather straightforward conservative approach to options trading, how to do it and what my expectations might be for the future (although there are no guarantees). I thoroughly enjoyed the seminar and I have never witnessed such an involved or attentive group of people eager to absorb the information you presented. I think that there is a lot more that I will learn because I intend to repeat the class exercise in detail. I am looking forward to seminars that you might present in the future, but next time I'll be bringing some of my relatives in tow so that they can learn the value of trading covered calls and naked puts.

Richard Short
Dunedin, FL

Many thanks to Ron and VISIONS software. He has shown me a solid way to improve my trading profits by 15%.

Don Watson
Tampa, FL

Ron's seminar presentation speeds up the learning curve. His covered call concepts and VISIONS searches all came together at the seminar.

K. M. Liebing
Naples, FL

Thanks Ron. This session of using computers was very beneficial to me. Being a hands-on person I have learned a lot more by actually pushing the buttons. I am leaving this session with the confidence that I can put Ron's fabulous formulas to work. Ron has put together some great stuff and proves it by his own experiences. It is amazing to me that he has put this software together with his own skills. VISIONS' easy access to information will be very helpful in my other trading practices as well. Thanks again.

Norde Wilson
Salisbury, NC

The Covered Call and Naked Put seminar held this past week was extremely informative. The seminar showed me how to better use the **VISIONS** software to prospect for qualified stock and covered call trades for my portfolios. I only wished I had known about this software several years ago. Ron's trading system is very easy to understand with a minimum amount of time needed to make a respectable monthly income. As a developer and programmer of specialized applications for clients, I have a great respect for Ron's programming efforts. This is a great stock research-trading system.

Richard
New Port Richey, FL

More comments begin on page 167.

Glossary

American Stock Exchange (AMEX). A private, not-for-profit corporation, located in New York City, that handles approximately one-fifth of all securities trades within the United States.

American Style Option. An option contract that can be exercised at any time between the date of purchase and the expiration date. The other type of contract is the European Style which may be exercised only during a specified period of time just prior to its expiration. Most exchange-traded options are American style.

Arbitrage. The simultaneous purchase and sale of identical financial instruments in order to make a profit where the selling price is higher than the buying price.

Arbitrageur. An individual that takes advantage of momentary disparities in prices between markets which enables one to lock in profits because the selling price is higher than the buying price.

Ask Price. The current cost to buy a security or option. It is the lowest price the seller will accept at that time.

At-The-Money. When an option's strike price is the same as the price of the underlying stock.

Automatic Exercise. The automatic exercise of an option that is in-the-money on expiration date.

Bare Cash. A companies cash plus marketable securities less long term debt.

Bear. An investor whose sentiment or belief is that a security or the market is falling or is expected to fall.

Bear Call Spread. A strategy in which a trader sells a lower strike call and buys a higher strike call to create a trade with limited profit and limited risk. A fall in the price of the underlying stock increases the value of the spread. This is a net credit (cash inflow) transaction. The maximum loss is the difference between the strike prices less the credit. The maximum gain equals the credit.

Bear Market. The stock market cycle where prices for the overall market fall for an extended period of time usually caused by a weak economy and subsequent decreased corporate profits. It is generally agreed that a bear market is when the stock market experiences a price decline of twenty percent or more, and lasts at least two months.

Bear Put Spread. A strategy in which a trader sells a lower strike put and buys a higher strike put to create a trade with limited profit and limited risk. A fall in the price of the underlying stock increases the value of the spread. This is a net debit (cash outflow) transaction. The maximum gain is the difference between the strike prices less the debit. The maximum loss is equal to the debit.

Bid Price. The current price you would receive if a stock (or option) is sold. It is the highest price the buyer will pay for that security at the present time.

Black Scholes Formula. A pricing model that is used by most options exchanges to price various options. It factors in the current stock price, strike price, time until expiration, current interest rates, and volatility of the underlying security.

Break-even. The price of an underlying security at which an option strategy neither gains nor loses money.

Bull. An investor whose sentiment or belief is that a security or the market is rising or is expected to rise.

Bull Market. The stock market cycle where prices for the overall market rise for an extended period of time usually caused by a strong economy and subsequent increased corporate profits.

Bull Call Spread. A strategy in which a trader buys a lower strike call and sells a higher strike call to create a trade with limited profit and limited risk. A rise in the price of the underlying stock increases the value of the spread. This is a net debit (cash outflow) transaction. The maximum loss is equal to the initial debit. The maximum gain is the difference between the strike prices less the debit.

Bull Put Spread. A strategy in which a trader sells a higher strike put and buys a lower strike put to create a trade with limited profit and limited risk. A rise in the price of the underlying stock increases the value of the spread. This is a net credit (cash inflow) transaction. The maximum loss is the difference between the strike prices less credit. The maximum gain is equal to the credit.

Buy Limit. The maximum price that should ever be paid for a stock, based on its 52 week low (L) and 52 week high (H).

$$\text{Buy Limit} = L + .25(H - L)$$

Buy Rank. A formula to rank the relative appeal of stocks on the prospect list. In the formula BL is Buy Limit, CP is current price, H is the 52 week high and L is the 52 week low.

$$\text{Buy Rank} = \frac{10(BL - CP)}{.25(H - L)}$$

Call Option. A contract that gives the holder the right (but not the obligation) to buy a specific stock at a predetermined price on or before a certain date (called the expiration date).

Chicago Board Options Exchange (CBOE). The largest options exchange in the United States.

Covered Call. A short call option position against a long position in the underlying stock or index.

Covered Put. A short put option position against a short position in the underlying stock or index.

European Style Option. An option contract that may be exercised only during a specified period of time just prior to its expiration.

Exercise. implementing an option's right to buy or sell the underlying security.

Exercise Price. See strike price.

Expiration. The date and time after which an option may no longer be exercised.

Expiration Date. The last day on which an option may be exercised.

Fundamental Analysis. Evaluating a company to determine if it is a good investment risk. Evaluation is based mainly on balance sheet and income statements, past records of earnings, sales, assets, management, products and services.

Go Long. To buy securities or options.

Good 'Till Canceled Order (GTC). Sometimes simply called *GTC,* it means an order to buy or sell stock that is good until you cancel it.

Go Short. To sell securities or options.

Holder. One who purchases an option.

Index. An index is a group of stocks which can be traded as one port-folio, such as the S&P 500. Broad-based indexes cover a wide range of industries and companies and narrow-based indexes cover stocks in one industry or economic sector.

Index Options. Call and put options on indexes of stocks that allow investors to trade in a specific industry group or market without having to buy all the stocks individually.

In-the-Money. An option is In-the-Money to the extent it has in-trinsic value. (See Intrinsic Value). A call option is said to be In-the-Money when the price of the underlying stock is higher than the strike price of the option. A put option is said to be In-the-Money when the price of the underlying stock is lower than the strike price of the option.

Intrinsic Value. A call option premium is said to have intrinsic value to the extent the stock price exceeds the strike price. A put option premium is said to have intrinsic value to the extent the strike price exceeds the stock price. The total value of the premium is intrinsic value (if any) plus the time value.

LEAPS (Long-term Equity AnticiPation Securities). Long dated options with expiration dates up to three years in the future.

Limit Order. A condition on a transaction to buy at or below a speci-fied price or to sell at or above a specified price.

Long. A long position indicates that a stock, index, or option is owned.

Margin. A loan by a broker to allow an investor to buy more stocks or options than available money (cash) in the account.

Margin Requirements (Options). The amount of cash an uncovered (naked) option writer is required to deposit and maintain to cover his daily position price changes.

Market Order. An order that is filled immediately upon reaching the trading floor at the next best available price.

Naked Call. See Uncovered Call

Naked Put. See Uncovered Put

NASDAQ (National Association of Securities Dealers Automated Quotations). A computerized system providing brokers and deal-ers with price quotations for securities traded over-the-counter as well as for many New York Stock Exchange listed securities.

New York Stock Exchange (NYSE). The largest stock exchange in the United States.

Option. A security that represents the right, but not the obligation, to buy or sell a specified amount of an underlying security (stock, bond, futures contract, etc.) at a specified price within a specified time.

Option Class. A group of calls or a group of puts on the same stock.

Option Holder. The buyer of either a call or put option.

Option Premium. The price it costs to buy an option or the price paid for selling an option.

Option Series. Call or put options in the same class that have the same expiration date and strike price.

Option Writer. The seller of either a call or put option.

Out-of-the-Money. An option whose exercise price has no intrinsic value.

Out-of-the-Money Option (OTM). A call option is out-of-the-money if its exercise or strike price is above the current market price of the underlying security. A put option is out-of-the-money if its exercise or strike price is below the current market price of the underlying security.

Premium. See Option Premium.

Price to Earnings Ratio (PE). The current stock price divided by the earnings per share for the past year.

Put Factor. A formula to guide the selection of a naked put strike price and strike month. A factor greater than one is desirable. In the formula, **PR** is the naked put premium, **SP** is the strike price, **CP** is the current stock price, and **ME** is months to expiration.

$$\text{Put Factor} = \frac{6\,(100\ \text{PR})\,(\text{CP} - \text{SP})}{(\text{ME})\,(\text{SP})\,(\text{SP})}$$

Put Option. A contract that gives the right (but not the obligation) to sell a specific stock at a predetermined price on or before a certain date (called the expiration date).

Security. A trading instrument such as stocks, bonds, and short-term investments.

Short. A short position indicates that a stock, index, or option is not owned.

Spread. The price gap between the bid and ask price of a stock.

Stock. A share of a company's stock translates into ownership of part of the company.

Stock Split. An increase in the number of a stock's shares with a corresponding decrease in the par value of its stock.

Straddle. A position consisting of a long call and a long put, or a short call and a short put, where both options have the same underlying security, strike price and expiration date.

Strangle. A position consisting of a long call and a long put or a short call and a short put, where both options have the same underlying security, the same expiration date, but different strike prices.

Strike Price. Also called the exercise price, is the price at which a call option holder can purchase the underlying stock by exercising the option, and is the price at which a put option holder can sell the underlying stock by exercising the option.

TAI - Take Action Indicator. Formula for determining the relative attractiveness of stocks on the prospect list. In the formula BR is Buy Rank, FDA is Fifty Day Moving Average and CP is the current stock price.

$$TAI = BR \left(1 + \frac{FDA}{2(FDA) - CP}\right)$$

Technical Analysis. A method of evaluating securities and options by analyzing statistics generated by market activity, such as past high/low, up/down volume, momentum and moving averages.

Time Value. An option's premium consists of two parts: time value and intrinsic value. (See Intrinsic Value) The time value portion of the premium deteriorates with the passage of time and becomes zero with the expiration of the option.

Triple Witching Day. The third Friday in March, June, September and December when U.S. options, future options, and index options all expire on the same day.

Uncovered Call. A short call option in which the writer does not own the underlying security.

Uncovered Put. A short put option in which the writer does not have a corresponding short position on the underlying security.

Web Site. An information location on the Internet. Each web site has a unique address called a URL that one uses to access the site and obtain information or transact business. The URL to download the VISIONS software is **www.RonGroenke.com**. The URL for Keller Publishing is **www.KellerPublishing.com**.

Writer. The seller of an option.

Appendix

*Now that you have gained the knowledge of the CA$H for LIFE concepts, your prof-
its will be greatly enhanced by specially designed software programs reviewed below.*

*The screen shots provided here are just a sampling of the power of
VISIONS, The Money Tree Tools, and the Stock Market Simulator.*

*You can experience this software free of charge by downloading and running a
trial copy from my web site* **www.Ron Groenke.com**.

VISIONS SOFTWARE: A STOCK AND OPTIONS SEARCH ENGINE. This dy-
namic program eliminates the drudgery of looking for the financial information for the companies that you might want to analyze and add to your
prospect list. The major functions are shown on the Start Page. Each button
below activates the function as named which are further described below.

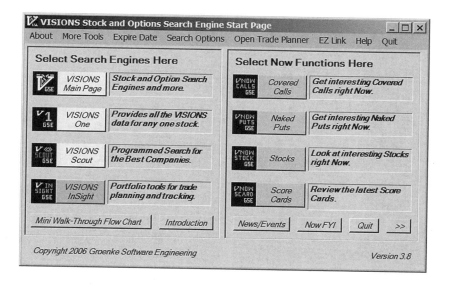

VISIONS SCOUT: AN AUTOMATED FULL STOCK MARKET SEARCH ENGINE.. With the touch of one button this search engine will search the entire stock market and return a list of the Top Ten companies that meet the ideal stock selection criteria as outlined in this book. This includes the fundamental financial analysis and the technical chart analysis.

Financial analysis looks at Market Cap, Revenue Growth, Quarterly Earnings, Revenue/Sales, Bare Cash, Volume of shares traded per day and Buy Rank. The technical chart analysis looks at where each stock is trading in relation to the VISIONS View V, Take Action status, and its Gold $ Score. Stocks that pass all the Ideal Criteria are candidates for the Top Ten list. The Scout Report shows the detail data for all the stocks passing the technical criteria and are shown in order with the Top Ten at front of the list.

There is nothing like Scout available in the financial community. It is unique and gives you the control to find the best investment opportunities right now any day any time.

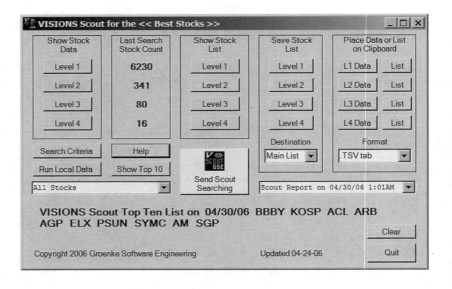

VISIONS SCOUT SEARCH REPORT

VISIONS Scout Report on 04/30/06 1:01AM

Print Find Calendar Throw Away 80 Entries

VISIONS Scout Report on 04/30/06 1:01AM

Company Name	Stock Symbl	Search Date	Quote	# Up Days	#Days In V	Gold$ Score	52Wk High	52Wk Low	50Day Avg	Buy Limit	Buy Rank	TA I@TAI	#Days	Best Fit	Beta	P/E	Div Yld$	Opn ?	Vol/ Day	Mkt Cap	Bare Cash	Rev/ Year	% Rev Gth/Y	Qtrly Erngs
BED BATH & BEY	BBBY	04-29-06	38.35	3	31	100	46.99	34.85	38.27	37.88	-1.55	TA	11	***	1.59	20.0	0	Y	3M	11B	851M	5B	14.8	++++
KOS PHARMACEUT	KOSP	04-29-06	48.40	3	25	100	78.40	40.90	47.15	50.27	1.99	TA	3	***	1.79	19.7	0	Y	729K	2B	412M	751M	41.9	++++
ALCON INC	ACL	04-29-06	101.71	3	19	98	148.70	94.44	105.58	108.00	4.63	TA	1	**	0.08	32.5	1.0	Y	1M	31B	1B	4B	8.1	++++
ARBITRON INC	ARB	04-29-06	35.66	3	17	94	44.76	32.68	33.88	35.70	0.13	TA	4	**	0.71	17.1	1.1	N	353K	1B	43M	315M	7.4	++++
AMERIGROUP COR	AGP	04-29-06	25.83	2	24	90	49.30	14.60	21.43	23.27	-2.96	WT	1	**	0.84	25.5	0	Y	508K	1B	402M	2B	26.5	++++
EMULEX CORP	ELX	04-29-06	18.15	2	20	90	22.68	15.06	17.46	16.96	-6.25	BI	1	*	2.43	21.2	0	Y	1M	1B	467M	425M	20.3	++++
PACIFIC SUNWEA	PSUN	04-29-06	23.30	3	14	88	27.99	20.33	22.45	22.24	-5.54	BI	3	*	0.47	14.0	0	Y	1M	1B	170M	1B	11.9	++++
SYMANTEC CP	SYMC	04-29-06	16.38	2	17	84	24.38	15.30	16.29	17.57	5.24	GR	10	***	0.59	98.1	0	Y	15M	17B	3B	3B	65.3	++++
AMER GREETINGS	AM	04-29-06	22.52	1	39	80	28.02	20.32	21.43	22.24	-1.46	TA	1	**	1.41	21.2	1.5	Y	553K	1B	322M	1B	3.7	++++
SCHERING PLOUG	SGP	04-29-06	19.32	1	26	80	22.53	17.88	18.91	19.04	-2.41	TA	2	*	0.30	67.1	1.1	Y	6M	28B	3B	9B	7.7	++++
ENDURANCE SPLT	ENH	04-29-06	30.96	1	26	80	39.69	29.00	31.50	31.67	2.65	TA	1	**	0.91	N/A	3.3	Y	453K	2B	20M	1B	1.1	++++
MEDTRONIC INC	MDT	04-29-06	50.12	3	9	78	59.87	48.77	51.45	51.54	5.11	GR	15	**	-0.01	30.6	0.8	Y	7M	60B	3B	11B	9.4	++++
JUNIPER NETWOR	JNPR	04-29-06	18.48	1	17	74	27.65	16.98	19.06	19.64	4.34	TA	1	****	2.50	31.4	0	Y	12M	10B	1B	2B	26.2	++++
LIFEPOINT HOSP	LPNT	04-29-06	31.70	1	17	74	51.54	28.27	29.98	34.08	4.09	TA	1	***	-0.26	22.1	0	Y	865K	1B	18M	1B	117.2	++++
GALLAGHER ARTH	AJG	04-29-06	27.44	3	6	72	31.94	26.07	28.01	27.53	0.61	TA	2	*	0.62	85.8	4.4	Y	636K	2B	847M	1B	2.3	++++
TIME WARNER IN	TWX	04-29-06	17.40	2	11	72	19.00	16.10	16.97	16.82	-8.00	BI	2	*	1.82	28.2	1.2	Y	27M	78B	4B	43B	7.0	++++
APOLLO GP INC	APOL	04-29-06	54.64	0	38	70	82.54	47.27	52.65	56.08	1.63	TA	16	***	0.77	21.5	0	Y	2M	9B	595M	2B	12.6	++++
YAHOO INC	YHOO	04-29-06	32.78	0	24	70	43.66	29.75	31.72	33.22	1.26	TA	8	****	1.19	26.4	0	Y	22M	46B	2B	5B	33.5	++++
LINCARE HLDGS	LNCR	04-29-06	39.53	0	19	68	46.00	37.63	39.07	39.72	0.90	TA	4	**	0.35	19.5	0	Y	728K	3B	47M	1B	9.3	++++
AMAZON.COM INC	AMZN	04-29-06	35.21	0	18	66	50.00	31.52	36.25	36.14	2.01	TA	15	****	2.94	45.3	0	Y	6M	14B	2B	8B	19.8	++++
JOHNSON AND JO	JNJ	04-29-06	58.61	0	18	66	68.87	56.70	58.98	59.74	3.71	TA	9	**	-0.06	16.2	2.3	Y	9M	174B	14B	50B	1.2	++++
AMER POWER CON	APCC	04-29-06	22.24	0	18	66	28.56	19.00	22.41	21.39	-3.56	WT	1	**	2.29	30.9	1.7	Y	1M	4B	773M	1B	13.3	++++
INVITROGEN COR	IVGN	04-29-06	66.01	2	7	64	88.50	60.14	68.36	67.23	1.72	TA	1	****	1.91	28.3	0	Y	707K	3B	751M	1B	24.0	++++
AMGEN	AMGN	04-29-06	67.70	2	6	62	86.92	57.12	71.21	64.56	-4.22	WT	6	***	1.20	22.0	0	Y	10M	79B	3B	12B	13.6	++++
GENENTECH INC	DNA	04-29-06	79.71	2	6	62	100.20	68.42	82.43	76.36	-4.22	WT	2	***	1.54	60.9	0	Y	3M	84B	282M	7B	35.9	++++

THE BUY RANK STOCK SCREENER SEARCH ENGINE. A fast executing search that looks at over eight thousand companies and selects those that meet your criteria for Buy Rank, Stock Price, Volume per day, and Market Cap. Retrieves the data for all companies and allows additional filtering and sorting. Once completed the list of stock symbols can be saved for use in any of the other VISIONS search engines. Your first step in finding great companies to invest in.

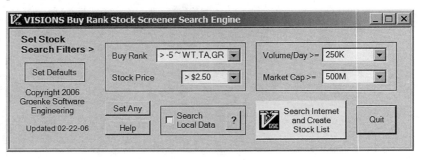

THE STOCK SEARCH ENGINE. A data mining machine that gets the data on any list of companies and finds the diamonds (companies with the highest best fit ranking) for investment consideration. It allows you to filter and sort the list to your specified criteria such as Buy Rank, Yearly Revenue Growth, Dividend Yield, PE, Trading Volume, Market Cap, Bare Cash, and many more. Searches can be performed on the supplied lists or on those you create and save.

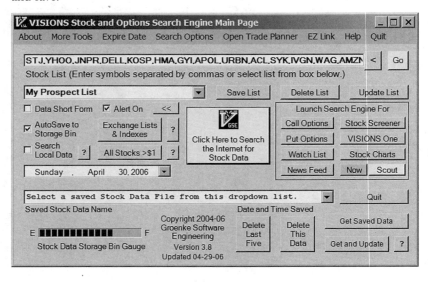

STOCK SEARCH RESULTS WITH FILTER PANEL.

From your VISIONS Storage Bin, AutoSave Results to Bin. AutoSave Results for List [SRCE,TW,COMS, 01-19-06 02:30 PM

Print Now Report Save Data Save Search Save Symbols Throw Away Set/Show Filters UnDo Sort Help Best Fit Key Help/Definitions Web Links BL/BR Wizard Data is Filtered

Company Name	Stock Symbl	Search Date	Quote	52Wk High	52Wk Low	50Day Avg	Buy Limit	Buy Rank	TA I	Best Fit	Best TA	P/E	Beta	Div Yld%	Opn ?	Vol/ Day	Mkt Cap	Bare Cash	Rev/ Year	% Gth/Year	Rev Qtrly Gth/Y	Qtrly Ermgs
VERISIGN INC	VRSN	01-19-06	22.30	33.36	19.01	22.24	22.59	0.80	TA	****	TA	23.8	3.49	0	Y	4M	5B	737M	1B	27.5		++++
W HOLDING CO I	WHI	01-19-06	8.94	14.18	7.31	8.45	9.02	0.46	TA	***	TA	10.4	0.54	2.2	N	524K	1B	973M	329M	10.6		++++
PLANTRONICS IN	PLT	01-19-06	30.36	41.01	26.40	29.27	30.05	-0.85	TA	***	TA	17.7	2.00	0.6	Y	538K	1B	242M	619M	32.3		++++
PACIFIC SUNWEA	PSUN	01-19-06	23.03	29.05	20.33	24.56	22.51	-2.39	TA	***	TA	14.6	1.22	0	Y	1M	1B	143M	143M	13.6		++++
P.F. CHANG'S C	PFCB	01-19-06	47.28	65.12	42.92	50.69	48.47	2.14	TA	***	TA	32.9	0.86	0	Y	570K	1B	70M	794M	16.7		++++
MITTAL STEEL C	MT	01-19-06	27.92	43.86	22.11	27.21	27.54	-0.70	TA	***	TA	4.4	1.51	1.4	Y	1M	19B	2B	27B	12.0		++++
LIFEPOINT HOSP	LPNT	01-19-06	31.89	51.54	28.57	36.42	34.31	4.21	TA	***	TA	20.7	0.00	0	Y	1M	1B	18M	1B	117.7		++++
KINDRED HEALTH	KND	01-19-06	28.33	42.11	24.74	26.83	29.08	1.72	TA	***	TA	9.2	0.33	0	Y	510K	1B	281M	3B	10.7		++++
INVITROGEN COR	IVGN	01-19-06	68.97	88.50	60.14	67.48	67.23	-2.46	TA	***	TA	33.9	0.63	0	Y	1M	3B	967M	1B	13.0		++++
HLTH MGMT ASSO	HMA	01-19-06	22.32	27.00	20.75	22.64	22.31	-0.07	TA	***	TA	15.8	0.00	1.1	Y	1M	5B	89M	3B	10.9		++++
COOPER COS INC	COO	01-19-06	52.72	84.70	44.75	51.47	54.73	2.01	TA	***	TA	26.4	0.00	0.1	Y	1M	2B	807M	2B	69.3		++++
CAREER EDUCATI	CECO	01-19-06	31.14	41.75	28.73	33.69	31.98	2.58	TA	***	TA	14.4	0.11	0	Y	1M	3B	331M	2B	14.1		++++
CABELAS INC	CAB	01-19-06	16.38	23.25	15.34	17.24	17.31	4.70	TA	***	TA	15.9	0.86	0	Y	397K	1B	85M	1B	12.0		++++
BED BATH & BEY	BBBY	01-19-06	37.10	46.99	34.85	39.38	37.88	2.57	TA	***	TA	20.1	0.98	0	Y	3M	11B	851M	5B	11.0		++++
AMER PHARMA PT	APEX	01-19-06	37.76	58.73	32.25	38.22	38.86	1.66	TA	***	TA	32.9	0.45	0	Y	717K	2B	67M	496M	34.7		++++

Visions Stock Filters [X]

A B C D E F   Get

Set these filters to the criteria for your search.

Select Favorite then Get to retrieve filter template.

Select Favorite, enter name, then set to save template.

Stock Symbols	Any
Stock Price	Any
Buy Rank (1)	Any
TAI (1)	=TA
Best Fit (1)	> blank
Beta	Any
Share Vol/Day	Any
Market Cap	>500M
Bare Cash	Any
P/E Ratio	Any
Div Yield	Any
Options Req'd	Any
Rev/Year	>250M
Rev Growth/Yr	> 10%
Qtrly Earnings	All 4 of 4

Do   UnDo   Set All to Any   Set   A   Do

THE STOCK CHART SEARCH ENGINE. Displays a 12 month view of the stocks on your list together with their Buy Limit, 30, 50, 100, or 200 day moving average, and comparison with the major indexes such as the DJIA, SP500, SP100, NASDAQ, or Russell 2000. Provides a take action indicator with number of days in the VISIONS View V. Charts are saved for use at any time.

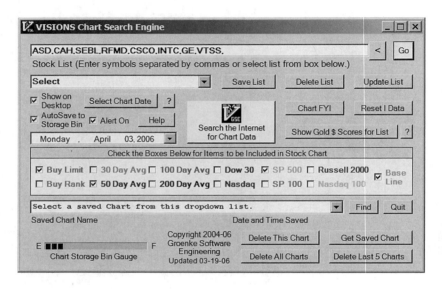

STANDARD CHART

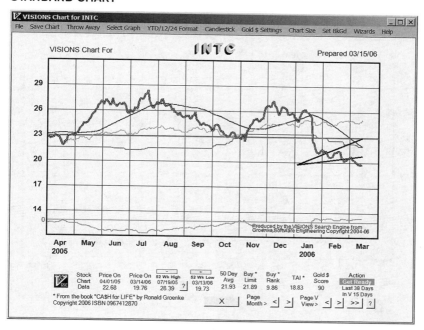

CANDLESTICK VIEW

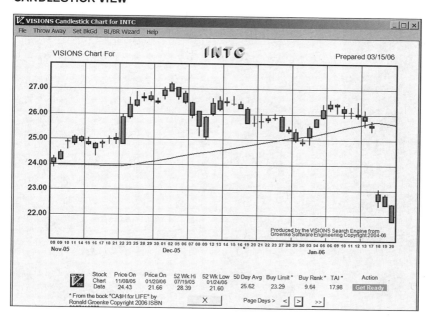

TWO YEAR VIEW

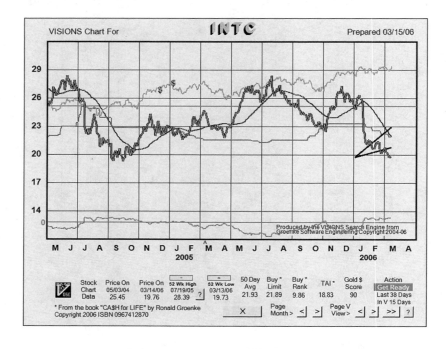

CHART GOLD $ SCORE REPORT. This report provides an ordered list of the best opportunities based on a chart analysis that calculates the Gold $ Score.

VISIONS Chart Gold $ Score Report

Print   Find   Calendar   Throw Away

VISIONS Chart Gold $ Score Report

Stock	# Up Days	# Days In V	Gold $ Score	Take Action Indicator	# Days At This TAI
BMET	3	23	100	Time to Act	8
APOL	3	18	96	Bad Idea	1
IR	3	17	94	Bad Idea	3
WAT	3	16	92	Wait	1
FDO	2	26	90	Time to Act	10
BSX	2	22	90	Time to Act	9
DG	2	24	90	Time to Act	6
ACV	3	15	90	Time to Act	1
INTC	3	14	88	Bad Idea	4
SYK	3	11	82	Wait	1
BIIB	1	28	80	Time to Act	20
MOLX	2	14	78	Wait	3
ALTR	2	13	76	Time to Act	4
COF	2	13	76	Bad Idea	2
APCC	2	11	72	Time to Act	10
PMCS	2	10	70	Time to Act	9
JNJ	2	10	70	Time to Act	7
BCR	2	10	70	Bad Idea	1
ORCL	1	15	70	Bad Idea	1
OMC	2	8	66	Bad Idea	14
LLTC	2	7	64	Time to Act	1
QLGC	1	11	62	Time to Act	9
MAR	2	6	62	Bad Idea	6

THE CALL OPTION SEARCH ENGINE. Displays the call options that meet your strike month, % gain, and premium criteria. It also provides the current price, the 52 week trading range, 50 day average, Buy Limit, Buy Rank, TAI, and Beta. A best fit to the Magic Chart is calculated along with percent gain for If-Sold and If-Expired, and months to expiration. Creates a summary of all the options sorted by best If-Sold % gain from all the stocks in your search list.

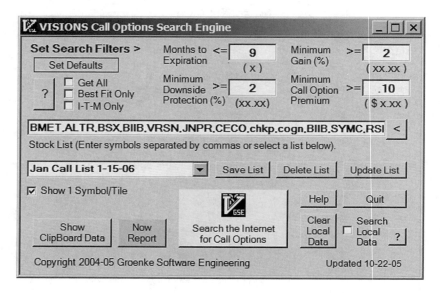

SAMPLE CALL OPTIONS FOR ONE STOCK INTC

Call Options for INTEL CP [INTC] On 01/19/06 10:42 AM Price < BL & 50DayAvg TAI=Time to Act
Price 22.71 (+0.11) 52WkHi 28.84 52WkLow 21.89 50DayAvg 26.04 BuyLimit 23.62 BuyRank 5.23 Beta 2.27

Option Symbol	Strike Date	Strike Price	Bid	Asked	Open Intrst	% Gain If Sold	% Gain If Exprd	% If Sold	% If Exprd	Mths Till Exp	Best Fit	Break Even Price	Down Side (%)	Bid/ StkPr (%)
NQBX	2/17/06	22.50	0.80	0.85	21,247	2.60	3.52	6.80	5.40	1		21.91	3.52	3.56
NQDX	4/21/06	22.50	1.40	1.50	19,082	5.24	6.16	10.00	8.00	3		21.31	6.16	6.22
INQDE	4/21/06	25.00	0.50	0.55	51,273	12.29	2.20	10.00	8.00	3	*	22.21	2.20	2.00
NQGD	7/21/06	20.00	3.50	3.60	1,862	3.48	15.41	14.80	11.90	6	*	19.21	15.41	17.50
NQGX	7/21/06	22.50	1.95	2.00	3,697	7.66	8.59	14.80	11.90	6		20.76	8.59	8.67
INQGE	7/21/06	25.00	0.90	1.00	8,283	14.05	3.96	14.80	11.90	6	*	21.81	3.96	3.60
VNLAC	1/19/07	15.00	8.20	8.40	3,387	2.16	36.11	24.40	19.70	12		14.51	36.11	54.67
VNLAW	1/19/07	17.50	6.10	6.30	23,815	3.92	26.86	24.40	19.70	12	*	16.61	26.86	34.86
VNLAD	1/19/07	20.00	4.30	4.40	17,873	7.00	18.93	24.40	19.70	12	*	18.41	18.93	21.50
VNLAX	1/19/07	22.50	2.85	2.90	20,673	11.62	12.55	24.40	19.70	12		19.86	12.55	12.67
VNLAE	1/19/07	25.00	1.75	1.80	47,851	17.79	7.71	24.40	19.70	12		20.96	7.71	7.00
VNLAY	1/19/07	27.50	1.00	1.10	40,708	25.50	4.40	24.40	19.70	12	*	21.71	4.40	3.64

CALL OPTIONS FILTERED AND SORTED FOR A LIST OF STOCKS

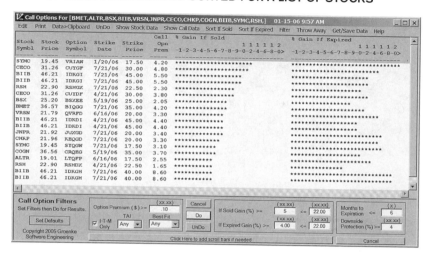

THE PUT OPTION SEARCH ENGINE. Displays the put options that meet your strike month, Put Factor, and premium criteria. It also provides the current price, the 52 week trading range, 50 day average, Buy Limit, Buy Rank, TAI, and Beta. A best fit to the Put Factor is calculated along with % discount and months to expiration. Creates a summary of all the options sorted by best Put Factor from all the stocks in your search list.

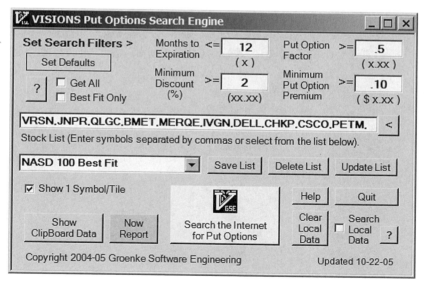

SAMPLE PUT OPTIONS FOR ONE STOCK SGTL

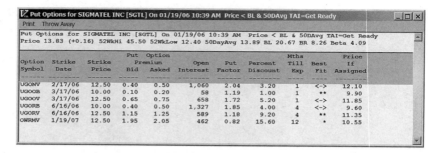

PUT OPTIONS FILTERED AND SORTED FOR A LIST OF STOCKS

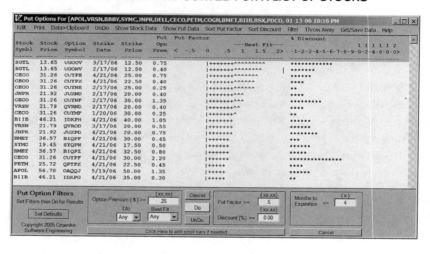

THE BUY LIMIT, BUY RANK and TAI WIZARD. This tool allows you to calculate the Buy Limit, Buy Rank, and Take Action Indicator for any stock.

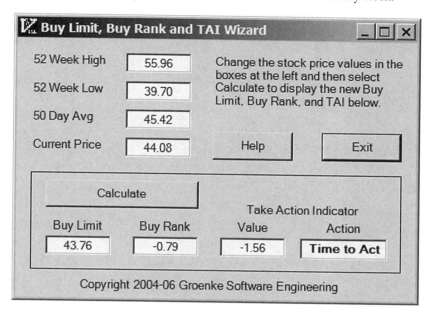

THE PUT ASSIGNMENT WIZARD. This tool allows you to calculate the probability of a Put assignment.

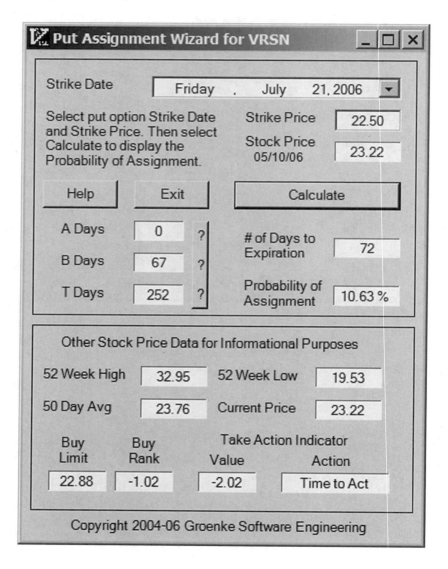

THE TRADE PLANNER. This tool allows you to prepare a plan for executing a number of Covered Calls and Naked Puts. You can review the overall results (% gain) on your current stock and option selections. You can save and print the plan at any time.

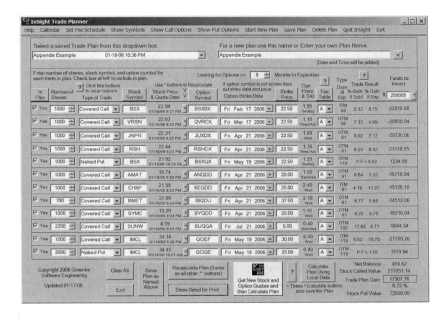

TRADE PLAN SUMMARY PAGE 1

```
VISIONS Trade Planner Detail Results                        _ □ ✕
 Print  Find  Calendar  Throw Away
VISIONS INSIGHT TRADE PLAN SUMMARY                        01-19-06

PLAN TITLE: Appendix Example                  01-18-06 10:36 PM

DATE      TRANSACTION                         (+/- AMOUNT)    BALANCE
--------  ------------------------------------- ------------ ----------
01-19-06  INITIAL INVESTMENT                  +  200000.00   200000.00

01-19-06  BUY 1000  BOSTON SCIENTIFIC CP  @  23.94  -   23945.00   176055.00
          SELL 10  BSX    FEB 22.50  CALLS @   1.95  +    1934.92   177989.92
          CALLED VALUE = 22480.04   SOLD % =  2.13  EXP % =  8.15
          BSXBX, ITM, TAI = GetRdy                 28 Days to Exp

01-19-06  BUY 1000  VERISIGN INC         @  22.03  -   22035.00   155954.92
          SELL 10  VRSN   MAR 22.50  CALLS @   1.10  +    1084.96   157039.88
          CALLED VALUE = 22480.12   SOLD % =  7.13  EXP % =  4.99
          QVRCX, OTM, TAI = Time2Act               56 Days to Exp

01-19-06  BUY 1000  JUNIPER NETWORKS     @  22.31  -   22315.00   134724.88
          SELL 10  JNPR   APR 22.50  CALLS @   1.60  +    1584.94   136309.82
          CALLED VALUE = 22480.11   SOLD % =  8.02  EXP % =  7.17
          JUXDX, OTM, TAI = Wait                   91 Days to Exp

01-19-06  BUY 1000  RADIOSHACK CORP      @  22.44  -   22445.00   113864.82
          SELL 10  RSH    APR 22.50  CALLS @   1.35  +    1334.95   115199.77
          CALLED VALUE = 22480.10   SOLD % =  6.28  EXP % =  6.02
          RSHDX, OTM, TAI = Time2Act               91 Days to Exp

01-19-06  SELL 10  BSX    MAY 22.50  PUTS @   1.25  +    1234.95   116434.72
          BSXQX, OTM, TAI = GetRdy, P F = 0.52     119 Days to Exp

01-19-06  BUY 1000  APPLIED MATERIALS    @  19.74  -   19745.00    96689.72
          SELL 10  AMAT   APR 20.00  CALLS @   1.05  +    1034.96    97724.68
          CALLED VALUE = 19980.21   SOLD % =  6.64  EXP % =  5.32
          ANQDD, OTM, TAI = BadIdea                91 Days to Exp

01-19-06  BUY 1000  CHECK POINT SOFTWA   @  21.55  -   21555.00    76169.68
          SELL 10  CHKP   APR 20.00  CALLS @   2.45  +    2434.90    78604.58
          CALLED VALUE = 19980.14   SOLD % =  4.18  EXP % = 11.37
          KEQDD, ITM, TAI = Wait                   91 Days to Exp

01-19-06  BUY 700   BIOMET INC           @  37.09  -   25968.00    52636.58
          SELL 7   BMET   APR 37.50  CALLS @   2.10  +    1454.94    54091.52
          CALLED VALUE = 26229.96   SOLD % =  6.77  EXP % =  5.66
```

APPENDIX

TRADE PLAN SUMMARY PAGE 2

```
┌─────────────────────────────────────────────────────────────────────────┐
│ ▓ VISIONS Trade Planner Detail Results                           _ □ x   │
├─────────────────────────────────────────────────────────────────────────┤
│  Print  Find  Calendar  Throw Away                                        │
├───────────────────────────────────────────────────────────────────────┬──┤
│01-19-06 BUY 1000  SYMANTEC CP          @  19.29  -     19295.00  34796.52│▲│
│         SELL 10  SYMC  APR 20.00  CALLS @  1.10  +      1084.96  35881.48│ │
│         CALLED VALUE = 19980.23   SOLD % =  9.38  EXP % =  5.70          │ │
│         SYQDD, OTM, TAI = Wait              91 Days to Exp               │ │
│                                                                          │ │
│01-19-06 BUY 2200  SUN MICROSYS INC     @   4.59  -     10103.00  25778.48│ │
│         SELL 22  SUNW  JUL 5.00  CALLS @   0.40  +       858.46  26636.94│ │
│         CALLED VALUE = 10980.60  SOLD % = 17.65  EXP % =  8.71           │ │
│         SUQGA, OTM, TAI = BadIdea          182 Days to Exp               │ │
│                                                                          │ │
│01-19-06 BUY 1000  IMCLONE SYSTEMS      @  34.14  -     34145.00  -7508.06│ │
│         SELL 10  IMCL  MAY 30.00  CALLS @  6.40  +      6384.74  -1123.32│ │
│         CALLED VALUE = 29979.63   SOLD % =  6.62  EXP % = 18.75          │ │
│         QCIEF, ITM, TAI = Wait             119 Days to Exp               │ │
│                                                                          │ │
│01-19-06 SELL 20  IMCL  MAY 25.00   PUTS @  0.80  +      1579.94   456.62 │ │
│         QCIQE, OTM, TAI = Wait, P F = 1.78  119 Days to Exp              │ │
│                                                                          │ │
│STOCK CALLED ASSIGNMENT VALUES AT STRIKE PRICE ON EXPIRATION DATE         │ │
│                                                                          │ │
│02-17-06 1000    BSX   CALLED @ 22.50        +     22480.04   22480.04    │ │
│03-17-06 1000    VRSN  CALLED @ 22.50        +     22480.12   44960.16    │ │
│04-21-06 1000    JNPR  CALLED @ 22.50        +     22480.11   67440.27    │ │
│04-21-06 1000    RSH   CALLED @ 22.50        +     22480.10   89920.37    │ │
│04-21-06 1000    AMAT  CALLED @ 20.00        +     19980.21  109900.58    │ │
│04-21-06 1000    CHKP  CALLED @ 20.00        +     19980.14  129880.72    │ │
│04-21-06 700     BMET  CALLED @ 37.50        +     26229.96  156110.68    │ │
│04-21-06 1000    SYMC  CALLED @ 20.00        +     19980.23  176090.91    │ │
│07-21-06 2200    SUNW  CALLED @ 5.00         +     10980.60  187071.51    │ │
│05-19-06 1000    IMCL  CALLED @ 30.00        +     29979.63  217051.14    │ │
│                                                                          │ │
│STOCK PUT ASSIGNMENT VALUES AT STRIKE PRICE ON EXPIRATION DATE            │ │
│                                                                          │ │
│05-19-06 1000    BSX   PUT ASSIGNED @ 22.50  +     22519.00   22519.00    │ │
│05-19-06 2000    IMCL  PUT ASSIGNED @ 25.00  +     50019.00   72538.00    │ │
│                                                                          │ │
│                                                                          │ │
│INITIAL INVESTMENT                       200000.00                        │ │
│STOCK CALLED VALUE AT STRIKE PRICE       217051.14                        │ │
│CASH IN ACCOUNT                             456.62                        │ │
│                                                                          │ │
│TOTAL PORTFOLIO GAIN                      17507.76                        │ │
│                                              8.75 %                       │▼│
└───────────────────────────────────────────────────────────────────────┴──┘
```

157

THE WATCH LIST SEARCH ENGINE. Displays the current stock price and daily change for any stock list. Can be set to run at the time interval you select such as providing an update every thirty seconds if desired.

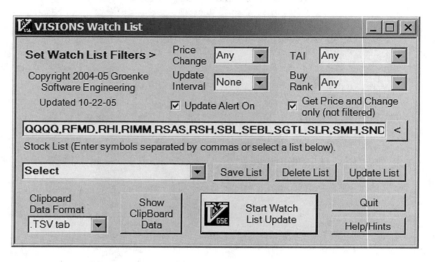

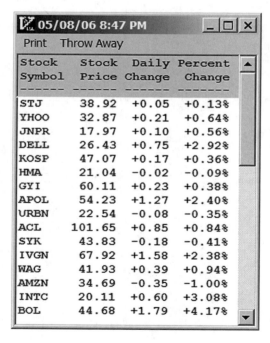

THE VISIONS ONE SEARCH ENGINE. Displays the Stock Data, Call Options, Put Options, and Chart for any one stock. Allows a quick look at all the information for any one company.

This is a small view. Run the free trial to see all the features in action.

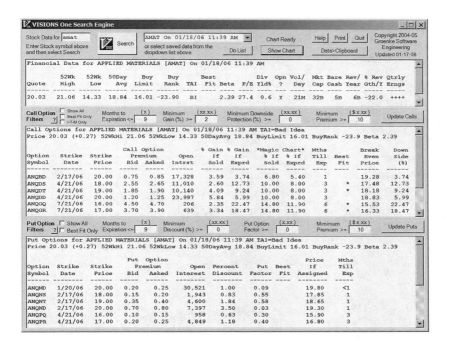

EZ LINK. This desktop panel provides quick access to any web site. You can setup the destination URL in a way that bypasses the ads and pop-ups. Save time and get to your sites in a wink with EZ Link.

VISIONS EZ Link (Copyright 2006 Groenke Software Engineering)						
VISIONS Main Start	VISIONS Call Options	VISIONS Put Options	VISIONS Charts	VISIONS One	VISIONS News	VISIONS Watch
VISIONS ScoreCards	Market Pulse	Market Snapshot	Market Summary	After Hours Volume Leader		
After Hours News	World News	The Wall Street Journal OnLine	WSJ Stock Quote	BrownCo Discount Broker		
Quote on all Nasdaq 100 Stk	The Nasdaq Stock Market	Nasdaq 100 Heatmap	Nasdaq EFT Heatmap	Pre-Mkt Nasdaq 100 He		
Chicago Board of Options Exch	Marketwatch Profile	Marketwatch Annual Income	MW Annual Balance Sheet	MW Annual Cash Flow		
MW Qtrly Income Statem	MW Qtrly Balance Sheet	MW Qtrly Cash Flow	Marketwatch Quotes	Marketwatch Options		
The Market and News Links	Bigcharts	Morningstar Markets	Yahoo Stock Profile	Yahoo Stock Screener		
Yahoo Stock Quote	Yahoo Stock Options	Yahoo Historical Stock	MSN Money Investing	MSN Money Stock Research		
MSN Money Stock Rating	MSN Money Stock Quotes	MSN Money Option Quotes	MSN Money Create Stk List	Zacks Investing		
Zacks Stock Research	Dogs of the DOW YTD Perf	Marco Island Beach CAM	Interactive Discount Broker	E-Trade Discount Broker		
Scottrade Discount Broker	Ameritrade Discount Broker	Harris Direct Discount Broker	Cyber Trader Discount Broker	Keller Publishing.com		
Blank	Blank	Blank	Blank	Blank		
Blank	Blank	Blank	Blank	Blank		
Blank	Blank	Blank	Blank	Blank		
Blank	Blank	Blank	Blank	Blank		

THE MONEY TREE TOOLS FOR WRITING COVERED CALLS AND NAKED PUTS. Provides Wizards, Worksheets, and other functions that allow you to quickly analyze any prospective call and put option prospect.

CALL OPTION WIZARD. Computes the gain (if called or if expired) from call premiums on various strike prices and expiration dates. Indicates desirable (Magic Chart) premiums.

PUT OPTION WIZARD. Computes the Put Factor for any strike price and strike month combination. This factor is then used to show the premium desired in your selection analysis.

PROSPECT LIST MANAGER. Computes Buy Limit, Buy Rank & Take Action Indicator (TAI) for stocks on your prospect list. Also sort by any column. Gets updates from the Internet when requested.

STOCK AND OPTIONS PORTFOLIO SIMULATOR. As described in Chapter 14, generates expected return for any account size, level of margin, call and put premium values and monthly, quarterly or yearly option cycles.

THE CALL OPTION WIZARD. Guides you in the selection of the proper strike month and strike price for maximum gain as shown by the Magic Chart.

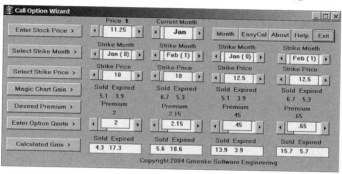

THE PUT OPTION WIZARD. Calculates the Put Factor for any strike price and strike month combination. This factor then is used to show the premium desired in your selection analysis.

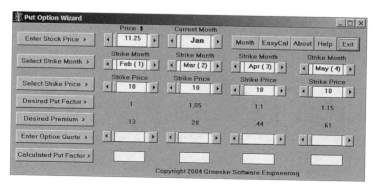

THE STOCK AND OPTION SIMULATOR. Allows you to review your plan for writing covered calls and naked puts. It gets you out of the dark and puts some light on the potential opportunities for your account. You can find out the difference between the potential gain for taxable and non-taxable accounts. Use it for covered calls or naked puts only or in any combination. This tool will show you how the compounding of option gains over time turns into excellent results in the long term.

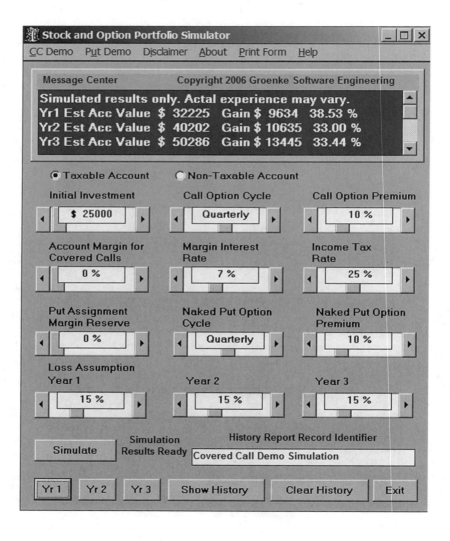

STOCK AND OPTIONS WORKSHEETS. Provides ready to use excel templates.

OPTION PLAN WORKSHEET. This worksheet lays out a month by month option plan by stock. Call and put premiums are totaled by month and year. Shows the yearly income potential from your holdings.

PROSPECT LIST WORKSHEET. Provides the stock selection criteria outlined in the book. Calculates the Buy Limit and Buy Rank for your prospects. Use the Excel sort function to sort on any attribute.

STOCK TRANSACTION AND HISTORY FILE Worksheet. Track your trades and summarize your results over time. Sort by stock to track results like the examples in the book.

THE MONEY TREE STOCK MARKET SIMULATOR. Allows you to forecast your own picture of where the market may be headed. It is based on your own assessment of things such as interest rates, the employment picture, GDP growth, and other factors. Track your forecast against the actual market performance over time. Use it as a guide for investment decisions.

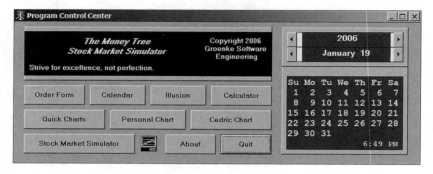

SIMULATE. Generates a forecast based on your factors. Provides tools for adding any stock or index to your database.

GRAPH. Prepares a graph of the forecast together with actual performance over a four-year period. Allows you to export the graph or data for additional analysis

APPENDIX

THE SIMULATOR PAGE. Allows you to select the factors that may affect the market in the future. After the simulation is complete the forecast is displayed. After reviewing the results you can change your assumptions or view a graph of the day by day result. . The Tools sections allows you to update the actual numbers for tracking or with the Build feature (if purchased), you can build your own model of a stock or index.

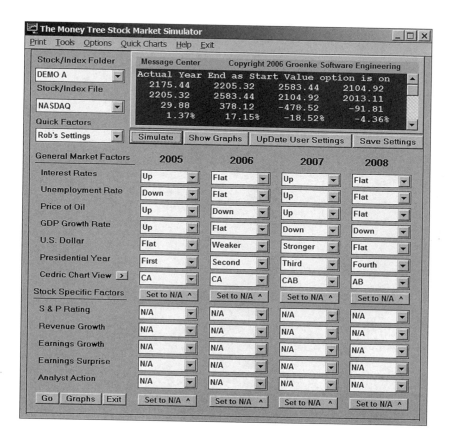

165

HERE IS A FOUR YEAR VIEW FOR THE FACTORS SELECTED. You can review results by year or multiple years. You can export any chart in data or bit map format.

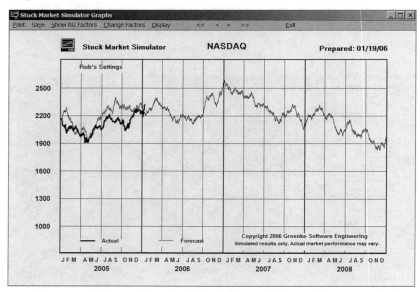

HERE IS A SINGLE YEAR VIEW.

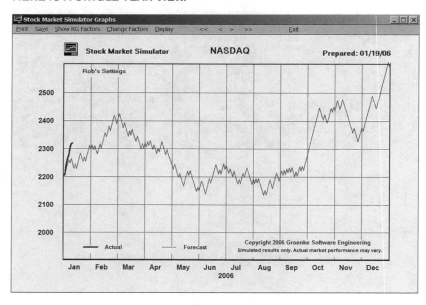

More Comments from Investors

After reading *Cash for Life* my Christmas shopping was done . . .
copies for all my money-tree-picking friends!

Tim Emish
Salt Lake City, Utah

As a finance professor, I am always looking for books that can
bridge the gap between academics and practice. Ronald Groenke
has written a practical book that does a great job of uncovering
the myths about options investing and making it appealing to an
individual investor. Most other books do a cursory job of covered calls
or just show the profit and loss diagram, leaving it to the reader to
figure out the rest. This book takes that concept and applies it using
real-world stocks and options, taking the reader through the various
possible states that he may encounter by taking the position. It is a
clearly written book that does not leave any unanswered question. I
strongly recommend the book as a supplemental text in financial risk
management.

Salil K. Sarkar, Ph.D., CFA
Associate Professor of Finance
College of Business Administration
The University of Texas at Arlington
Box 19449, Arlington Texas 76019

Cash for Life is an excellent book that puts in a very enjoyable
and readable format the beauty of the options market as part of a
complete investment strategy. I highly recommend the book as an
interesting and practical explanation of the options market for both
the novice and the experienced investor who wishes to broaden their
investment opportunities.

Dr. Richard Rawlins, PhD
Professor Finance & Economics
Missouri Southern State University
Joplin, MO 64801

I found *Covered Calls and Naked Puts* [Ron Groenke's second
book] on the shelf at a bookstore and was thrilled by the idea of
being able to generate a reliable income from my portfolio holdings.
The story told in the book easily conveys the financial concepts
behind the stock market and was my first exposure to call and put

options. My interest in implementing my own money tree led me to find an excellent on-line brokerage house for trading calls and puts (ThinkorSwim). I can't wait to find the time to attend a VISIONS workshop on Marco Island!

Amber Lhamo M.Ed.
Talent, OR

I started an investment plan using the *Cash for Life* concepts in Nov. '05. It has generated cash every month. I also recommend using VISIONS software because it does all the heavy lifting in evaluating the "Time to act winners."

Dan Mellon
Ohio

I have been trading—albeit not always covered calls—for more than twenty years. Ron's method, described in his latest book, *Cash for Life*, is one of—if not the—most understandable and easy to follow trading method that I have seen. Every concept is described in easily understandable language and each step detailed in easy to implement order. I have been using Ron's method for over two years and have had much more success with it than any other search engine. Compared with other covered call search engines costing far more (and I have used them) the VISIONS software is the most powerful in my opinion and it is a great time saver.

Stan Graham
California

I have purchased multiple copies of Ron Groenke's first two books, *The Money Tree* and *Covered Calls and Naked Puts.* I have given them as gifts to friends because I believe the strategies Ron teaches can lead to financial freedom. The VISIONS software is a powerful tool for locating stocks that are perfect for covered calls and naked puts. I highly recommend *Cash for Life* and VISIONS software!

Mark Casey
Texas

DON'T buy *Cash for Life* UNLESS you want to make money trading stocks and options! Groenke's basic philosophy of making small gains consistently is the name of the game. Slow and steady wins the race! And VISIONS software makes it easy to find the right stocks and options. Do yourself a favor: Buy *Cash for Life*, follow its principles; watch your account balance grow dramatically in only a few months. I use the book as the primary text in a Financial Freedom class I teach; it's terrific and my students love it!

Richard Goudeau
Macon, GA 31210

Ron has developed a conservative approach to using options to increase your gains. His approach is based on years of experience in trading covered calls and the use of naked puts to enhance returns. I have read a large number of investment books and Ron's methods are the best that I have seen for a practical approach to success in the stock market. I highly recommend *Cash for Life*.

Tom Tompkins
Minnesota

I have found *Cash for Life* to be the most complete and easily understandable book on covered calls. Combine that with VISIONS software and one has a comprehensive strategy to make money with options.

L.K.

I have found that Ron's system works. Of course any system is very dependent on 1) picking the right stocks and 2) having the discipline to cut your losses by honoring your initially-set stops. *Cash for Life* and VISIONS software have been a great help in doing just that.

Paul Vorndam
Rye, Colorado

Ron's software and book can teach you how to plant your own money tree, which is even better than a nest egg, because trees keep on growing long after the egg has been scrambled.

T J Gaynor
Chicago, Illinois

I read *Cash for Life* last night. Congratulations! Have not enjoyed an academic book this much since reading *The Goal* by Goldratt 15 years ago. I found myself into the story, wanting to get a pencil and paper, find a calculator, grab a *Wall St Journal*, and get to work making money. The story line is subtle and believable. The covered call explanation is clear and a logical development of the formulas. The examples blend into the construction of the total theory of making money via covered call technique. This could he a "How to . . . " book or an academic supplement to a hedging/financial instruments course.

Dr. Bob Cluskey
CPA, Professor of Accounting
State University of West Georgia
Carrollton, GA

I have read innumerable books regarding the market. Of the dozens of books I have studied, I personally feel that *Cash for Life* is the best written and most useful text I have employed in my trades over the last 10 years. I have used the VISIONS Software on a monthly basis to assist in picking my covered calls and naked puts candidates. Of all the trades I have made while using this software, I have only lost money on one trade! Amazing! I would like to thank you for all the help your publications have given me in continuing my development as a successful trader!

Bob Anderson
Murray, Utah

Cash for Life is a very readable introduction to these low-risk strategies for producing an income stream from one's portfolio. The methodology is sound, well explained in the book and well implemented in the software. The book, the software, and Ron's seminar are great values.

Chris Walker
California

Ron has distilled a complex subject into easy to understand tools and methodology for generating a regular cash flow from stocks that you already own.

Roger Hay
Morgan Hill, CA

Meet the Author

Ronald Groenke

RON GROENKE moved from Minnesota to the sunny Gulf Coast community of Marco Island after twenty-five years in the communications systems and software development environment. He has been active in the stock options market for twenty years and developed the concepts and techniques provided in the book.

On Marco, he and wife, Jean, are active in their church and busy entertaining family and friends who visit from the north.

Besides options investing/advising, Ron's other activities include personal computing, Rotary, walking, boating, and traveling.

Ron can be reached at **robgrahamphd@aol.com**.